JULIE CHRISTIE

ACKNOWLEDGEMENTS

Many people directly and indirectly inspired and supplied this bio-filmographical work. Some graciously granted interviews, others delved deep into forgotten files. Others still won my affections and gratitude by giving encouragement. I owe special thanks to Tony Crawley, film expert extraordinaire and voice of my conscience, and of course to my tireless editor, Hilary Muray. I'm also grateful to my parents Michael and Margaret. Also to: Leslie Phillips, Michael Hayes, Chris Menaul, Jane Judge, Frederic Albert Levy, Joan Brown, Peter Vollebregt, Gayle Hunnicutt, Brian Keogh, David Farrell, Christopher Cormack, Carolann Manahan, Morgan O'Sullivan, Conor Hourigan, Susan Cooper at the Birmingham Repertory Theatre, Linda Wood and Mary Jane Walsh at the British Film Institute, Dr Levi Fox of the Royal Shakespeare Company, Simon Crocker and Alex Lascelles at Kobal, and the information and library staff of the many journals researched. Although Julie Christie has not been involved with the writing of this book, I have accurately reported and I hope faithfully reflected what she has said to other journalists and writers over the course of her career.

For midnight support – too rarely mentioned – I am grateful to the Wilsons, the Gibbs, Jacinta and Ree. This book is fondly dedicated to them all.

Michael Feeney Callan

W.H. ALLEN · LONDON

Photographs are reproduced with the kind
permission of the following:

p. 14 *Sparrowtree*
pp. 6, 49, 53, 104, 106, 108, 111, 113, 133, 140,
144, 145, 152, 174 *Tony Crawley*
p. 19 *Michael Hayes*
p. 41 *Birmingham Repertory Theatre*
pp. 159, 160, 179 *Christopher Cormack*
p. 172 *British Film Institute*

All other photographs, including colour pictures,
are courtesy of *The Kobal Collection.*

Extracts from *Snakes and Ladders* by
Dirk Bogarde reproduced by kind permission of
Chatto & Windus

Typeset by Phoenix Photosetting, Chatham
Printed and bound in Great Britain by
Mackays of Chatham Ltd, Kent
for the Publishers, W.H. Allen & Co. PLC
44 Hill Street, London W1X 8LB

ISBN 0 491 03303 6 (W.H. Allen hardcover edition)
ISBN 0 86379 023 2 (Comet Books softcover edition)

CONTENTS

EMBRYO

YOU STAND IN a nondescript tributary of the Bayswater Road, London. A cluster of anonymous names tag the bell studs. Beyond the black panelled door a hallway filled with bicycles opens to uncarpeted stone steps that lead to her door. No one answers your call. You wait, and ruminate on the legends and the yarns.

'Her last apartment was incredible,' says David Farrell, a stills photographer who covered one of her most recent films. 'A huge room, a football field, stretching from a dining area to a bathroom with nary a screen in between.' You remember her well-reported domestic odyssey of the sixties and seventies, filled with rebellions and discoveries. She never liked reporters, resented their pursuit from hotel to lodging house. Granting interviews seemed like a betrayal of truth, because she had to resolve her own mystery. Twenty years later she still resents interviews, and for many the mystery widens.

In Wales, the Wales beloved of her deceased mother, she has a home too. It's a grey stone farmhouse near Powys where afforestation is extensive and Kerry Hill sheep are indigenous. On her straggling upland acres a dozen black sheep roam. In the makeshift stable there is a chestnut mare, occasionally pestered by an errant Tamworth pig or two. Her immediate neighbours – few and very far between – speak fondly of her. 'There is no one like Julie. I have never had a better friend in my life.' But Julie isn't here either. In residence are Jonathan and Leslie Heale, dear friends, artist friends – most recent in a line of compatible intimates who share the chores and guard the gate.

Upstairs, somewhere, in a hatbox in the dank attic, is the jewel and *bête noire* of her life: an inscrutable valueless gilt figurine called Oscar that marked the apotheosis, the moment an immature, unready actress was plunged into stardom. The movie was *Darling*, a central fragment of the dazzling mosaic that was the hedonistic subculture of the sixties. Julie's role enshrined unbridled, amoral sixties' youth, executed so well that the image lingers even now. And so – her friends say – she

In *Billy Liar*

flees from the old image and its obligation, extending that gypsying spirit, unscrambling the skeins of falsehood, searching for herself.

In 1965 *Newsweek* was trilling:

> In an industry where so many sweet young things go begging unless they have good connections, a suddenly sensational British actress named Julie Christie seems to have the very best there are – mysterious connections with the breeze, which tosses her hair, and with the sun, which clears her way along a crowded street . . .

The very week this feature was published the 24-year-old subject of *Newsweek*'s rhapsodizing, the 'slightly angular atavist', was crucially ill, and exhausted from the pressures of four major movies in two years. *Newsweek* reported her blithely arriving in New York to promote *Dr Zhivago,* moving with flagrant zest, buoyed like a sailplane by invisible currents, swinging her pop-art purse – the incarnation of the pluckiest girl in the happiest Beatles song.

Years later Christie would reveal with an anguished candour that the forced hyping tour: 'knocked me out. I could think of nothing but wanting to go to bed and sleep for ever and never talk to anyone again.' She was ill daily: 'I never felt so drained . . . I'd lost so much weight that the doctor was getting worried.' But *Newsweek,* whose agents had stalked her for months, was, in the spirit of the decade, more concerned with hyperbole than analysis. She was, they said, neither Mod nor Rocker, but Mocker. She was 'tough, radiant, gay, distracted and irresistibly alive'. Yes, in some ways she appeared uninvolved with flitting fashionability, though perfectly attuned to her time. And yes, she was nervous: photographers could expect blurred results, since her hands were always shakily reaching for the next cigarette or combing through her blonde mane. She was no great talker, and her smile was often enigmatic, forced.

The years since *Darling* and the beginnings of fame have been, for all to see, professionally, domestically and romantically difficult. There have been good films, unexpected films and, not infrequently, bad films. There have been dispiriting, headline-hugging love affairs. Her crusading for social and political causes has been trivialised in the pop press, although she has been involved in serious debate about apartheid, American Cruise missiles in Britain and press and broadcasting freedom. After a period away from the limelight her recent films have included critical successes like *Heat and Dust,* for which Christie returned to India, where she was born, to explore the half-remembered images of her childhood and challenge her own mysteries. Twenty years on Julie Christie is not the dip-lipped Darling of the sixties, the tousle-haired sex bomb. Her image is subtle and fresh, something extraordinary, beyond the manufactured 'enigmas' of showbiz, and it masks a personality that is bewitchingly elusive.

Julie Christie is not, as a thousand journalists have learnt to their great annoyance, the possessor of a good or even reliable memory. Recollections of her childhood in India could be scribbled on the back of a postcard and are distinguished only by the hunch that even then she probably wanted to be an actress. She was born on the 900-acre tea plantation her father managed in Assam, in the north-east of India, bordering Bangladesh (formerly East Pakistan) on April 14, 1941 – a time of upheaval in the valleys and plains. During World War II Assam became one of the main supply routes for Allied forces operating in Burma and within the territory decisive battles were fought in 1944 which effectively blocked the Japanese invasion of India. The Christies' plantation was far removed from the action, however, and the main concerns were more often sorting out problems with the immigrant Nepalese and Mongol work-force and fighting the monsoons.

By colonial standards the Christies were, apparently, no more than comfortably well-off. In an area where ninety per cent of the population were deemed remote rural dwellers and villages were (and are) far scattered, the gravity of close family life tended to become a special binding force. Yet Julie, even as a very small child, resisted. Obstinate independence goes as far back as she can remember. Her only anecdote, the only faithfully repeated story from that era, is revealing: 'One day my *ayah* (native nanny) took me out into the garden and tied me to a bush with a leather belt . . . I was a pretty naughty child most of the time, I suppose. She told me tigers would come and get me . . . I was scared out of my mind, and I never forgot the incident.'

Schooling was minimal, friendships few. The *ayah* taught her ward some Assamese but the inevitable insularity of an only child on a large plantation in a foreign land took its toll. Independence went hand-in-glove with introspection, outward strength with inward insecurity. More than once in the future Julie would pass off her childhood as 'mostly unsettled, unhappy.' Julie's mother had already resolved for her a course of education and a life away from India and in 1947, the opportunity came to visit England, the Christies' true home. Rosemary Christie regularly recalled the child's early artistic flights of fancy. Julie stole clothes and make-up and practised mimickry at a very early age. 'Mum told me I used to say I wanted to be an actress,' Christie says. 'I wish she was alive today because I've often wondered how, in the middle of Assam, I could have known *anything* about acting . . .' But she does remember the dressing-up, and games of the imagination with baby brother Clive who arrived on the scene some time later.

Formal schooling began in Bexhill, Sussex, under the guidance of a retired childless couple, pen friends of Rosemary Christie, with whom the seven-year-old child lodged after Rosemary's return to Assam. (In fact, Rosemary had advertised in newspapers for a couple to look after Julie.) At first there was day school, but Julie was recalcitrant and boisterous and a phase of 'school-hopping' began where the restless child was shuttled through no less than five schools. The surrogate parents must have wept oceans, but the strain was no less for unhappy Julie who 'loved them deeply'. About every three years Rosemary Christie visited, renting a house at Cuckfield, Sussex for months on end in a single-handed attempt to maintain some continuity of family life.

Brother Clive was brought to England for schooling too, and settled rather quicker. But Mrs Christie was displeased with her daughter's progress. There was no real attempt to acquire self-discipline or learn, and Julie still indulged her wayward imaginativeness. 'She thought up rather grim things,' Rosemary Christie later reported. 'Not sweet little stories about elves and fairies, but things about poor, suffering Victorian boys.' The only affectionate interest she displayed was for the company of cats, never dogs. Gradually brother Clive cracked the shell and grew close to her: 'I remember dressing up a lot with her. We had a sackful of wonderful costumes from India. Later, when she was eleven or twelve, we started playing cricket together . . . She was extremely good, always hitting the ball right out of the ground.'

The coiled energy, most believe, grew from inner contradictory impulses: Julie loved her foster parents – 'especially Aunt Elsie' – but was aware of a kind of unreasonable displacement. She was undeniably precocious – though she veiled her intelligence behind bluster – and probably foresaw the break-up in Rosemary's marriage. 'She always treated her family well,' Clive stressed, but: 'She was openly naughty, there was nothing insidious about it.' Julie played no games with herself; she simply did and said what she wanted to, and suffered for it when she had to.

Boarding school solved no problems, so Rosemary put her into a convent school where, curiously, total transformation occurred – albeit temporarily. Julie entered her religious phase – which, again, lasted not too long. She was expelled for telling dirty jokes. 'I don't remember what they were,' she told the *Sunday Telegraph*. 'I was thirteen and extremely childlike . . . my mum was upset, but she thought it silly too.' Her next sally was just as reckless. At yet another school she narrowly missed expulsion after tucking her uniform dress into the waistband of her knickers and parading for the delectation of the local boys. In fact, the day was hot and the act had been performed in all innocence – but Julie suffered a grim admonition, and the memory rankles even today: 'Can you imagine how damaging that was? – to force young girls to be so self-conscious about sex. As a result I *fantasised* about boys all the time, though in fact I found mixing with them difficult.'

There was some improvement at the next Sussex academy – sufficient to evoke happier reflections and an admission (to *Woman's Own* in 1981) that, behind it all, she learnt to enjoy her school days. At a Bexhill day school life became quite normal for a gutsy, fit-of-limb fifteen-year-old: 'Boys, my red swagger coat, red shoes, little red pochette, shocking pink lipstick – a far cry from boarding school.' And yet she didn't consider herself attractive, felt she must paint herself up and pretend. Once, she recalls, she was invited to a party. 'I was too shy so I muttered excuses about not being able to go.' But the girl issuing the invitation was distressed because she had promised to bring along 'this beautiful girl friend'. Christie was astounded: 'Beautiful – me! No one had ever said that before and I was convinced it couldn't be me. But the girl meant it . . .!'

She studied hard, had fun and advanced to a school at High Wycombe, Bucks, where she pulled seven satisfactory 'O' levels from the hat but drastically disappointed her mother by failing French. 'We had to write a story entitled *Un jour dans l'espace* which was supposed to be about a journey into space. I thought it meant a day in the country.' In punishment, Rosemary despatched her at once to France, to stay with friends, a large and rather unconventional French family – 'frenzied intellectuals and decaying aristocracy,' Christie describes them – at Tarbes, Gascony, near the foothills of the Pyrenees.

The initial impact of yet another alien culture, more strangers, renewed isolation, shocked Christie profoundly. In her first warm summer at Tarbes she was desperately ill-at-ease, vacillating between rage and outright, abandoned panic. She wrote repeatedly to Rosemary, begging her to relent. She wanted no more upheaval in her life: the butterfly glimpse of contentment in the last months at Bexhill and High Wycombe she wanted to ensnare, enshrine, keep forever. But Rosemary held no illusions about adolescents. She herself had led a hard life, was suffering the pangs of a failing marriage. Her weaknesses would never be Julie's. She wrote back tersely, simply stating that, from her experience, it would be wrong to allow Julie home. One of Julie's letters entreated: 'Please let me come home, another week will KILL me.'

And then, in the way of things, in the sudden snap when adolescence breaks to some kind of maturity, Julie was suddenly reviewing her prospects differently. Total separation from family meant freedom and the termination of schooling was, at least, in sight. When she reappraised her surroundings they showed some promise: 'I suddenly found myself living with a *wonderful* family – very intellectual and sophisticated about life. The father was writing a dictionary of the Basque language – and they were all so damned eccentric . . . They used to fly into great family rages and shout at each other, and of course I had been used to stuffy English restraint . . .

They were like something out of a novel by Colette and the house was brocaded and . . . wonderful.' Julie made her first close female friend, another deserted English girl and, overnight, in her words, life turned to 'absolute bliss'. Homesickness, indeed any dream of hoped-for home stability, became flickers in the gloom of the past. Passions quickly developed, inspired by the French: a love for history and classic art.

'As a child I think of myself only as an embryo,' Christie later said. 'Life really began when I went to France . . . I came straight into contact with the bits of life you never know about in English schools.' In Gascony there were boys, charming, randy, persuasive French boys, knowledgeable about art and loving, eager to teach. There were grand balls, food feasts, sparkling wines – the perfect romantic atmosphere for a brimming, eager dreamer to choose her course and set sail. In a year Julie's horizons broadened immeasurably. The first tentative, never-to-be-fulfilled love affairs began – all smuggled kisses and earnest, silly trysts – and she hatched her first tentative dreams of a career.

At seventeen she was on her way back to Britain, fluent in French, with a hand-grip full of trendy clothes and a few new dreams. When she'd left she had, she said, felt like an empty vessel. In France the vessel filled. 'My mind started going voom, voom, voom.'

She came home, observers noted, 'under the spell of dangerous foreign doctrines: men, love, beauty, love, art, love.'

She might, she reckoned, go on to university to read history. She might become an artist. Another remoter consideration seemed less accessible but more fun. She mused about the doorway into acting.

A FOR . . . ACT ONE

Around the time of *Dr Zhivago,* probing her own past, Julie Christie rummaged through a drawerful of old photos and letters in her Kensington flat. She found a picture of a young Richard Burton, a dashing, dark-eyed publicity handout. Maybe, fanlike, she had written away for it, maybe she borrowed it from a school chum. On the back was scrawled: *Please don't touch. Very private property. Very precious property.* The signature appended was 'Bugs', her juvenile pet name ('because I was like Bugs Bunny, I talked too much'). Her creaky old memory mechanism stirred and days later she was able, untypically, to recall for a visiting journalist some formative theatrical inspirations. Yes, she had taken parts in school plays and relished the experience. One of her sparkiest roles was as a cavalier. 'I had to make a great swashbuckling entrance with big boots on. Then I had to sit down at a table, slam down a tankard and *shout* about something . . . I *loved* it.' More importantly, from early on, the magic of top class professional theatre entranced her. She had been just a tot, she recalled, when her mother took her to see Burton in his favourite part, Shakespeare's *Coriolanus* at the Old Vic. She thought him marvellous and sat spellbound as he slunk around the stage as the Roman traitor, aloof and fascist, carving what Olivier believed was 'the definitive Coriolanus'. Such hero-worship, muted as it was, may well have started her very gradual move towards personal ambitions for the theatre. Friends are equivocal: she was a football fan too, and 'raved about' a variety of field stars.

At any rate some time during the year after her return from Gascony a very cool and assured decision to enter theatre was made. She took her 'A' levels at Brighton Technical College – without tantrums or disasters – and promptly joined the essential coffee bar set. Serenaded by the rattle of espresso machines and the skiffle of the jukebox and seduced by her first 'real boyfriend', a sensitive

In *A for Andromeda*

leather-clad hunk called Joel, Christie sketched an optimistic scenario for her new life: she would go to drama school, graduate to rep and hope for a break into the West End big time; in between, most probably, she would starve. Joel encouraged her. Her tawny looks and coltish legs were the stuff of silver screen stardom, he was sure. She was someone to be seen with, and the other bar boys envied him. Still little more than a kid, she had a cheeky hauteur about her that came from travelling the world; she could speak fluent French (and still some Hindi) and her clothes were exotic.

Her precocity could easily have made her unpopular in this fiercely competitive adolescent mating setting – especially with other girls – but she had engaging ways, weaknesses that glaringly stood at odds with her new maturity. An actor who drifted briefly through her circle recalls: 'She wasn't timid by any means, but she was shy. She liked to hang in the background and you got the impression she was happier with her private thoughts than in open chat or debate. She was distant . . . and that was often exciting.' Years later, at the height of her star exposure in Hollywood, bitching columnists would reiterate this, observing her 'quiet retiring presence' at boyfriend Warren Beatty's parties.

Hollywood was light years away from off-season Brighton and the critical decisions of the winter of 1957. For now all Julie Christie wanted was a flat of her own and a job. Sussex she loved, but the lure of Cuckfield diminished by the day. She kept in close, affectionate touch with Clive, and with her mother, but after France she was desperately eager for full-blooded independence. Less and less she slept at home. Instead, in her own words, her 'air-mattress era' was about to begin. She trekked from flat to flat, 'crashing in' on a variety of cafe chums, sleeping on the pumped-up bed in any available corner. Another associate of that time says, 'She loved company, just being among students and happy people . . . it was a craving.'

Under Joel's guidance she auditioned for the Bristol Old Vic and, at the same time, the Central School of Drama based at the Embassy Theatre, in Swiss Cottage, London. To her amazement – and obvious great joy – she passed both auditions and was offered simultaneous places. With little hesitation she accepted the Central School, attracted more by its situation in London than any worthier criteria. She'd had enough of the provinces, she told friends, and, as the affair with Joel fizzled, saw little reason not to swap the dingy seatown cafes for brighter city lights. 'I never seemed to meet anyone *interesting*,' she later grumbled. And, with that imperious, French-originated edge: 'Any boys who wanted to take me out had to have cars and be prepared to drive about eighty miles (to London) and back.'

Already the jaws of hungry ambition were opening.

* * *

Drama school training was twice as tough as Christie anticipated; equally it was twice as rewarding. She gypsied to London with the blessing of her mother ('she didn't mind one way or the other: you can't stop a child doing what it wants to do') and assiduously applied herself to imitating the romantic unconventionality of those decadent French. She dressed in the currently fashionable uniform of bohemianism – fisherman's jumpers and all-purpose slacks – aligned herself with a string of 'mates' (a perennial favoured word of hers), and acquired a new hobby – cooking. She had some financial support from home but she was, mostly, flat broke – just like her mates.

For more than a year she had no one place of residence, so the air mattress and cooking recipes jaunted from room to room once again, more often than not ending up squashed into the dustiest corner of some rundown indigent's hideaway in the Swiss Cottage area. For one particularly lean period of many months, Christie recalls, every night meant a new hovel. But she wasn't in the slightest deterred. On the contrary, roughing it seemed to bring out the formidable best in her. All her shyness was dispelled and the nervous outbursts of her earlier years abated. She herself said: 'My biggest problem (then) was terrible, terrible shyness and gaucheness which always made a lump come to my throat when I was, say, at a party . . . particularly with the opposite sex.' Michael Hayes, the eminent television director who was to spot Christie at Central and break her into film work some two years after her studies began saw none of this. To him, from the moment they met over coffee in the summer of 1960 she was, quite simply 'strong'.

'It was the middle of 1960 and I had a fine, promising TV series in development for the BBC,' Hayes told me. 'They were excellent scripts by science writer Fred Hoyle and John Elliot which predicated the use and abuse – and risks – of giant computers. In the way producers work I put out word that I needed a stunning, unusual girl for my central character, the female lab assistant. I wasn't especially looking for someone new, just someone fresh, utterly captivating – and of course capable. Then an agent rang me, can't recall his name, bless him – but he had a fine idea. He was enthusiastic about what he called 'the English Brigitte Bardot at Central'. His enthusiasm, to give him credit, fired me.'

Hayes went along to an end-of-term student matinee at the Embassy – one of the many where producers and agents were invited to survey the new crop of graduates. The production was a superbly low-key drama in which Christie was prominently spotlighted as heroic Anne Frank, the Dutch Jewess whose *Diary* recorded the experiences of her family in hiding from the Nazis. Hayes was impressed and immediately made an appointment to meet and discuss possibilities with her. By coincidence, unknown to Hayes, another important director viewed the *Anne Frank* production too. He, like Hayes, was currently contracted to the Beeb and speculating on future projects. Unlike Hayes, he found Christie's performance sadly lacking – but he remembered her face and her name, and mused on her chances. His name was John Schlesinger, former actor, at that time primarily a maker of documentaries, but destined in time to partner Christie to major movie success.

Hayes met Christie and liked her: 'more in person than on stage, I'll admit.' Within a few minutes he had made up his mind to cast her in the prestige seven-part series, to be screened at prime time. 'She wasn't fazed by this success,' says Hayes, 'and success, for a drama school pupil, it surely was. Others would have given their right arm for the part. She had an air about her that told you this was a logical progression from study to film work.'

When she was told the part was hers she responded calmly and conveyed the word in like manner to her mates. Some, naturally, were jealous. Others reckoned her 'apparent indifference' evinced a colossal lack of awareness of the minefield that was showbiz. She simply wasn't aware how freakishly lucky she'd been. True, she had already started the TV audition trail and had had the rejections but Hayes's series, *A for Andromeda,* was to be, by the standards of the day, a blockbuster. Anyone involved had struck good gold.

A for Andromeda was shot over eleven weeks – four on location in Pembrokeshire, seven in quasi-live studio in London. Its transmission, early in 1961, brought a deluge of approving letters into the Beeb. 'Julie deserved the success,' Michael Hayes says. 'Whatever stories about diffidence or awkwardness one might hear, well, they never affected us. She was perfect for the part. From such a young girl I hadn't expected that quality of enormous strength . . . more precisely, self-containment.'

Andromeda, in the style of Nigel Kneale's *Quatermass* hits of the fifties, was an instant cult winner. Cambridge Professor of Astronomy Hoyle, and writer Elliot, devised a clever plot where earthlings, trustingly following instructions from outer space, build a sinister computer. Once completed, it sets about mastering the world. Christie, the lab assistant, is killed and resynthesized as a blonde android. (She wore a brunette wig for the early sequences as indeed she had done when Hayes, and Schlesinger, first saw her in *Anne Frank*). The question then arises: which master will the android serve – her flesh-and-blood old lover or the inhuman alien mastermind? Philip Purser, the critic, thought the philosophic proposition – will science triumph over man, or can man contain science? – decently done. 'The answer,' he wrote, 'came excitingly after a rather lumpish start and the ideas were . . . of quality.' The value of Christie's contribution was explicitly expressed. Reviewing *Andromeda* in

Halliwell's *Television Companion* Purser concludes that 'a sequel lacking Julie Christie, *The Andromeda Breakthrough,* also lacked comparable impact.'

As it happened, *Andromeda* marked a major career transformation for Christie. Within weeks of being cast a clutch of other welcome offers was thrown her way. Rediffusion offered her a plump part in a J.B. Priestley play and Frinton-on-Sea rep company invited her aboard. Clearly the drama school dividends were coming faster than any young actor, no matter how naturally talented, might reasonably have expected. 'She was, in as far as you can judge about anyone,

Julie Christie through the lens of her first director, Michael Hayes

naturally talented,' Michael Hayes believes. Though, in fairness, he adds, 'there wasn't an awful lot of acting scope in *Andromeda,* not in any taxing sense.' Probably, he agrees, Christie's looks provided the immediate lure. 'I photographed her a lot myself,' he says, 'being a dab with the old hand camera. Even now I have the shots our stills man took in Wales during filming – outstanding black and white day-for-night shots [exposure adjusted to give a nightlike look]. My God, you couldn't take a bad shot of her . . . this full-mouthed, square-jawed vixen, with the most luminous large eyes.'

Her personality, as the crew of *Andromeda* remember, was easy going though, one man reports, making friends with her wasn't all that simple. 'She could draw into herself very quickly, grow very aloof.' Michael Hayes made friends with her, supped with her, even took her to the movies. 'She was good, chatty company,' he says.

At Central she was admired, though not as popular as bubbly extroverts like, say, Elizabeth Bell, a fellow student who found a career in TV. An associate says: 'Liz was in the same class as Julie . . . another actress of splendid potential. Comparison is unkind but suffice it to say that while Julie *was not cold* in the general social scene, Liz was warm.' The truth was, Christie preferred a social life a little removed from Central and the pressures of learning the craft and role-hunting. By her own admission designers and painters were more acceptable than actors or theatrical agents, because they offered no direct competition. 'By the time she made Frinton,' says Hayes, 'she had a lay-your-ears-back determination to make good.'

But after the burst of successful television work there was – equally suddenly and surprisingly – an arid, jobless period. The graph of progress quickly took a downward curve, and Christie was deeply shocked. Frinton continued to offer her patchy stage work but ambitious auditions went suddenly sour. Her agent continued to swing good interviews, but the end results were always negative. Harry Saltzman and Albert Broccoli, then in heated preproduction on *Dr No,* first of the Bond movies, were persuaded to consider her for the lead role of Honey Rider, prototype Bond-heroine, opposite Sean Connery.

Director Terence Young, the man generally credited with moulding the enormously successful Bond series, had selected Christie from scores of contenders – indeed, she had been sent to him by agent Laurence Evans of MCA, the man who handled Ian Fleming's film affairs. 'She was an absolute knockout,' Terence Young says warmly. 'I was mad about her.' She sat through many impressive readings for Young and eventually accompanied him to the producers' Mayfair office for a thorough, final read-through. Saltzman was delighted but Broccoli, though he admired her dramatic sense, had reservations. Later that day he told his partner: 'She's great, but she's no good for us.' When Saltzman queried him Broccoli came back pithily: 'No tits.' The role went to breasty Ursula Andress, a very average Swiss actress who built a towering career on her success alongside Connery.

Other film-makers came tantalizingly close too. Director Michael Winner screen-tested her for his breakthrough *West II*, but failed, like Young, to sway producer Daniel Angel who judged her 'a B picture actress.' Celebrated Italian producer Joseph Janni – famous for *The Glass Mountain* (1948) and *A Town Like Alice* (1956) – was casting Stan Barstow's classic *A Kind of Loving*, a movie he had high hopes for, when he agreed to audition Julie. Months before he, like his acolyte John Schlesinger who was slotted to direct the new movie, had seen Christie at Central. 'I was impressed,' Janni later said, 'and invited her round to my office.' But the subsequent in-depth interview proved unsatisfactory with Janni sadly deciding 'there was nothing here for her . . . but I told her: one day we must make a picture for you.'

Director Schlesinger had had the opportunity to watch Christie in an assortment of activities at Central over many weeks. While shooting a documentary called *The Class* for Huw Weldon's BBC *Monitor* programme, Schlesinger observed her interestedly. She did not appear in *The Class* but some indefinable magic drew Schlesinger to her, though still he insisted her talent was lacking. 'She was,' he said quite flatly, 'not ready.' In the event June Ritchie and Alan Bates piloted *A Kind of Loving* to a Berlin Festival Golden Bear Award and a place in British film history, slated as the finest film of the tail-end phase of the Angry Young Man era.

Christie, meanwhile, went back on the boards, jockeying for the best parts she could get in anything at Frinton – straight drama or revue. Her floating group of impoverished mates kept her spirits buoyed but indignities were frequent. For a start there was the galling sense of personal blame for failure to maintain the initial momentum. Then there was what one director calls 'the nightly calamities of half-cocked rep'.

'One of my most embarrassing moments happened during a play called *Live Like Pigs*,' Christie remembers. 'There were about one hundred short scenes and you really have to have your wits about you and remember when you were on or off stage. Well, I got mixed up. Suddenly the house lights began to fade and there I was in the middle of a scene I should not have been in. I just curled up on the floor and pretended to be a rug. The actress in that scene . . . who was supposed to be seducing the man next door, nearly died of shock. . .'

Julie could laugh, and her laughter kept her fundamentally optimistic and sane. Other distractions helped too. In her attic flat, after a night on stage, she often sat with her mates and speculated, like legions of bright kids before her, on issues like world peace. 'She was well read,' says an actor friend, 'and history was her first and deepest love. But she wasn't only a talker. She was a doer.'

'I'm not a great one for causes,' Christie reported in *Woman* around that time. 'If you look at most of these things there are two sides to the arguments.' At a service to commemorate Human Rights Day, however, she appeared at the Church of St-Martin-in-the-Fields in Trafalgar Square, in company of actor friend Cy Grant. Both wore handcuffs, symbolizing the millions of people imprisoned throughout the world for their radical beliefs. Apropos of the two-sides-to-every-argument comment she said, 'There doesn't seem to be another side to sticking people in prison for what they believe. There are a lot of people in that situation in Portugal, for instance . . . very sad.'

But she emphasized again her 'simply human interest'. She was no campaigner.

In the spring of '62, after the squalls of the previous breathless year, life levelled out and a career upswing started again. A new attic apartment 'with potential' in Earl's Court was found, and Christie moved in with her favourite four artist friends of the moment. Massive redecoration that kept her happily scouring backstreet junk shops brought her tranquillity – and tranquillity, as it always seemed to do in her early life, brought attendant success.

Director Ken Annakin, on the crest of a gigantic popular cinema wave with his recent *Swiss Family Robinson* (1960), was plotting his return to comedy with a Leslie Phillips-Stanley Baxter vehicle, *Crooks Anonymous,* scheduled to be the first of three loosely-linked feature romps. Annakin had seen Christie in *Andromeda* and had noted her recent new career departure – spread through trashy glamour magazines in leggy, innocuous pin-up poses. Not unreasonably he, along with the inspired production team of Julian Wintle (later famous for *The Avengers*) and Leslie Parkyn, focused on the workable possibilities of this 'new Brigitte Bardot' rumour. Christie was called to Beaconsfield Studios, to be interviewed and put through her camera paces. 'It wasn't a foregone conclusion that she'd be cast,' says Leslie Phillips, the definitive screen comedian of the British Golden Era. 'I was close to Leslie [Parkyn], indeed he became a kind of career father to me, bless him – and these films were to be built more or less around me. Julie was a special interest case, yes. But the director and producers interviewed scores of girls because the parts proposed in the scripts were substantial enough. I sat in on those interviews and remember vividly Julie's arrival.'

At the first interview Christie was edgy, but Phillips makes it clear she was 'afraid of no one'. She spoke up for herself and gave every indication of enthusiasm. Like Hayes, Annakin was impressed by her

With Ken Annakin, director of *Crooks Anonymous*

all-weather photogenic quality. She was bright, good-humoured and fresh-looking – but still some members of the interview panel had reservations. 'There were endless, endless discussions about *her bottom lip,*' says Phillips frankly. 'Some of us thought, it's too big, too noticeable, she'll look awful on film, it's not the look of today. Which was nonsense, of course, because these very features – the eyes, the large mouth – were the things that made her, her trademark features as time went on. But it's easy to be wise *after* the event.' Phillips and Parkyn did like her 'obvious sexiness. She had something that made you look twice. There was a touch of arrogance about her – which can be very sexy in some women, and it worked for her.'

After weeks of haggling a fat multi-picture contract was offered by Parkyn: the female lead in *Crooks Anonymous,* with 'new star' billing, and at least two other features over the coming few years, for distribution through Rank. The deal was good, the film company ultra-respectable, the cash badly needed to sustain the Earl's Court flat. Conceivably too, Christie liked to know that she was wanted and felt the need to test herself again, urgently, in film. She accepted Parkyn's offer and started *Crooks Anonymous,* her first movie, almost immediately.

Within weeks the prepublicity handouts from the studios had her smouldering: 'I want to have men go dotty over me. And I'd like to have *longer* legs and shorter hair. And I'd like to be famous so that when I walk down a street in Italy or Spain people will turn round and stare and know who I am. . .' But by the end of the year, and after a second film under Annakin, her tune had changed. She was repeatedly reported saying: 'Certainly it's nice to be making money when most actresses my age are in rep. I've been paid, I'm grateful. But if this is all my face leads to, I'll break my nose and start over again.' The threat was brassy, and ungracious. But it came with such ferocious cold passion, in such sudden contrast to the sexy brainless image Annakin was projecting, that people were shaken.

Leslie Phillips defends Christie: 'It's understandable I suppose. No one lived under false beliefs about what we were doing. *Crooks Anonymous,* for instance, was a nice little film – and that's all it was. An entertainment, no more. But while we were at Beaconsfield *This Sporting Life* was also shooting there. I remember the general feeling was: that one will get the 'crits' [good critical notices] and we'll make a fortune. Which, in the case of *The Fast Lady,* the second film with Julie, was precisely true. But we all *wanted* to be in *Sporting Life* – that's just the natural instinct, the way of our business. We all *want* to be in the best. And Julie, from the beginning, was like that.'

During the six-week shoot Christie was often 'slightly miserable' but even depression worked a perverse charm on her, making her, according to Phillips, even more sultry-looking. 'She didn't openly argue with anyone – but at twenty or whatever one tends to be headstrong and unreasonable. Certainly she had a natural aptitude and, for me, there was absolutely no strain working alongside her –' He chuckles darkly – 'until I had to bed her [in the film]. But there was the odd not so good day. Once or twice she . . . well, seemed to stay up all night, which made her working life a little harder than needs be.'

Annakin, a very controlled and strong director, was patient and encouraging with Christie – to a point where some people were surprised by his forbearance. Parkyn for his part steered clear of the set, always eager to avoid confrontations and rows unless troublesome incidents or people looked likely to hinder progress. 'But the situation was always in control,' says Phillips. 'On occasion Ken sent Julie home. She was tired and he'd say to her: get some sleep. But that was about it. These people were professionals . . . and they liked dealing with professionals. Leslie [Parkyn] was the kindest of men, nature's gentleman. Neither he nor Julian were dealers in horseflesh. They had Julie on contract but they were sensitive to her feelings. All right, she may have thought she wasn't starting right – that her movie career should begin in a different area – but at least she was up there, getting her break. Still, there was no sense of do-or-die-by-the-contract. Yes, I think they tried to *make her* like a star. They tried to groom her, with the benefit of their expertise and experience. But they understood she had ambitions beyond Beaconsfield. . .'

Christie was most offended by the exploitation of her sexuality, the non-stop drooling, pouting, posturing that seemed improperly untaxing, no different from shooting miles of moving pin-ups. She worked under sufferance, but all the while she dropped the hints, alluding to her greater ambitions.

Within a short time movie-makers, if not movie-goers, began to sit up in their seats.

LUNN'S
KING-FLIGHTS
KING-TRAINS
MAJORCA
ITALY
SWITZERLAND
KING-CRUISES
FRANCE
BULGARIA

IN AND OUT OF AMBROSIA

John Schlesinger has always maintained, eloquently, not always circumspectly, that Julie Christie was no great shakes to begin with. There were aspects of her face, her features, her presence, that never quite suited the moment, the mood or any part he ever considered her for. At Central in *Anne Frank* she simply 'wasn't terribly good', in his assessment. In magazine glamour spreads she looked fine but in the flesh, made-up with similar lascivious intent, she appeared 'awful' to him. In Annakin's frothy *Crooks Anonymous* he called her 'pretty dreadful' and opted not to sit through a full screening. In the circumstances, it seems more than a miracle that Schlesinger even in late '62, was teetering on the brink of adopting her like a new surrogate father and making her an international star.

Crooks Anonymous, to be fair, wasn't all bad. Leslie Phillips took top billing as Forsdyke, a pathological petty thief who subjects himself to a strict correction course run by a wealthy ex-con and his Crooks Anonymous organization. Christie played Forsdyke's virginally exquisite girlfriend Babette – in name and nature a too-obvious derivative of B.B. herself – who holds hopes for her man's recovery and dangles the carrot of marriage. In the end, having endured all sorts of agonizing tests conducted by the splendidly-named Widdowes (Stanley Baxter), Forsdyke loses control when locked in a department store over Christmas and, with the help of a gaggle of fellow reformers, makes off with a fortune from the safe. Babette, however, brings them to heel and insists that the loot be returned.

The black and white photography is uninspiring (in Christie's case oddly unflattering) and silliness of the *Carry On* camp sort abounds but, as the *Monthly Film Bulletin* observed, 'some sequences (notably Baxter's) reveal real ingenuity and lunatic flair.' It went on: 'Though by no means blessed with subtle wit, this film does not disgrace the novel idea that supports it.'

As Liz in *Billy Liar*

Not surprisingly, Christie's notices were patronizingly banal – just exactly what the publicity handouts invited. A notable exception was Leonard Mosley in the *Daily Express*. He, for one, glimpsed beyond the affectation of Babette. 'It used to be,' he wrote, 'that every time a producer read a story with a good fat part for a young British actress, he would throw it away. Young British actresses of talent simply did not exist. I am pleased to announce that things are improving, and so are the girls. This week I have had an advance view of a new girl with looks, poise, personality and potential. Her name is Julie Christie and at twenty-one she is a girl to watch.'

Christie might have drawn strength from such encouraging reviews

Offset on *The Fast Lady*

but their effect was double-sided. Independent Artists, the Parkyn-Wintle company, had her for three pictures and was sufficiently pleased with the comedic flair of *Crooks Anonymous* to keep ploughing the same waters. Parkyn was sharp enough to know when he was onto something good: without doubt there would be more Phillips-Baxter-Christie rib-ticklers. Like it or not, Christie was trapped. An actor associate recalls: 'It was, in her eyes, a bad luck break. She'd been broke, had had a tough time getting parts – so she jumped at the Annakin films. At Central she'd been turned down for a grant because her father's supposed income was high. And that was ironic because she had no cash, couldn't get any . . . and wouldn't have begged her family anyway. So she kept her decent values and just set out to legitimately earn some cash. I don't know if she'd seen the scripts [of the Annakin films], but the contract was definitely good money, and that was all she cared about at the start.'

In spite of Leslie Phillips's observations, bitter conflict with Independent did, apparently, develop quite fast. Somewhere along the line Annakin's and the producers' patience snapped. During the making of a second film, a grander, better-written farce called *The Fast Lady* – ('It cost £300,000,' says Phillips now; 'a fortune – and exactly the same amount I saw spent on a 30-second commercial I made last week!') – Christie was reprimanded for her insouciant individualism. She was earning enough money, the producers reckoned, and yet she showed up at Beaconsfield on a rusty scooter.

Weeks later she was reproved again when she wore a severe grey suit – 'copied from the French,' she proudly claimed – to a press showing of the first film. 'I thought the suit was wonderful,' Christie complained. 'But they said it was all wrong, that I should wear black. I told them I'd give up films first. I like money and what it can buy – clothes mostly. But I don't want to be part of any organization that I cannot control.' If, as Phillips believed, Parkyn wanted to groom her in the conventional way for star exposure the extent of her willing participation was no longer in question. 'I don't want a secretary or a chauffeur or a maid because then you become responsible to them and you cannot move without them. I want to be free.'

The confusion of ideals, which really only underlined a painful lack of self-understanding, was manifest in photo sessions of the time. The fanzines had her willingly semi-draped, pouting, deep of cleavage and void of subtlety. She *looked* like a star fully fledged. And yet the captions groused: 'I'm starlet, spinster, a pretty face, everything I feel but an actress. I want to stop being just an itch for the circle.' Profound? Truly meant? Even Christie wasn't sure. To some colleagues she spoke of extended ambitions in Annakin-type movies, of her great good fortune. To others – boldly to the press – she was restless to get free from Independent.

'I've never really thought about being a star,' she told *Woman*, 'I'm not even sure I want to be one. I came into this business because I want to act and I seem to be running before I can walk. I haven't even put a foot on a professional stage yet. Do you realize that? Not one foot!' Perhaps, as someone has suggested, she just disliked the set-up at Beaconsfield, the Hollywood-moguls manqué, the dying throes of the British studio-centred system.

Whichever way, by New Year 1963, she had resolved to get out. The overwhelming success of *A Kind of Loving* sealed the partnership of long-established Jo Janni and movie-newcomer John Schlesinger. They were to go forward into the Swingin' Sixties as one of the film world's most adventurous and outstanding producer-director teams, image-makers and iconoclasts both. In late '62, having completed the Barstow film, their attention had turned to *Billy Liar,* a book and stage success for writer Keith Waterhouse and (in the stage and film adaptation) Willis Hall. Early casting was straightforward – Tom Courtenay, who'd played the role on stage, as Billy; Wilfred Pickles and Mona Washbourne as the much-suffering parents who quarrel with his fantasies. One part, however, teased the patience of both

With Leslie Phillips (left) and James Robertson Justice in *The Fast Lady*

men: neither could readily think of anyone suitable for Liz, the self-reliant wanderer who urges day-dreaming Billy to escape to the Big City far away from dreary Bradford.

After weeks of studying actor directories both men, simultaneously by most accounts, came upon the idea of borrowing the glossy glamour girl from Independent. Janni's and Schlesinger's versions of the 'discovery moment' differ. Janni said he saw Julie's picture on a magazine cover, idly passing the time on a train to Bradford and decided, 'That's her, that's Lizzie.'

Schlesinger recalls different circumstances. Both men were in Janni's office three floors above Bruton Street, Mayfair. 'We were discussing the girl we wanted for Lizzie, a sort of earthy mother figure, a heavily-breasted all-enveloping creature . . . I saw this magazine, [the now defunct *Town* magazine], this girl on the cover and a series of photographs inside. Very good pictures, very provocative. She looked scrumptuous, absolutely marvellous. I didn't connect the girl with Julie as I remembered her.' A quick call was put through to Christie's agent and she hurried to Bruton Street for a reading with Tom Courtenay. Interviewed by the press much later Christie stressed her absolute conviction in the necessity of capturing the part though her feelings at the time, according to colleagues, were probably vaguer. It is clear though, in the wake of the highbrow acclaim for the stage version, that she saw the prospect as a likely antidote to a long life in light films.

Christie arrived in Janni's office looking her scintillating best. She had recently snatched a short holiday in Cunit, Spain – her first ever real holiday – and looked tanned and rested. Schlesinger was initially impressed, as was the breezy, effusive Janni. The ensuing test reading, however, was bad. Christie was nervous, oppressed by the company, distracted by the recent dictates of Annakin, unsure of this director's requirements. Schlesinger wasn't too disgruntled despite everything but Janni, as he always did, insisted on further tests. 'Jo never trusted the first try,' Schlesinger reported. 'The very idea of readings bores him.' And so Christie was taken out to location, to screen test with a couple of other long-shot hopefuls in the freezing winter air of Hampstead Heath and Waterloo Station. Pressured for time because of continuing work on *The Fast Lady*, she faltered again: 'I did a bad reading and followed it by three very bad screen tests. I don't let myself expect things, certainly nothing as enviable as this would have been, working with the man who had just made *A Kind of Loving*.'

Returning to Beaconsfield after a day of relaxed inventive direction from Schlesinger was heartbreaking. 'I tried not to let myself hope for the part,' Christie said. 'But after *three* tests you can't help hoping. I wanted desperately to do some respectable work . . . something I wasn't ashamed of.'

But when the rushes of Hampstead Heath were run Schlesinger was displeased. Gruffly he confessed, 'She was not quite what I was looking for. Funnily, she came over very cold . . . not at all *happy.*' He swiftly, cautiously added: 'She still looked good though – indeed, too good to be true.'

The source of unhappiness, in retrospect, is patently obvious, and might have been to the sagacious Janni: a compound of unease with Independent and the nervous hope most relatively inexperienced actors suffer at big auditions. Though she hadn't openly confided her pent-up confusion, Janni could read between the lines. Schlesinger – on the evidence of her screen tests – wanted to reject her, but he too sensed some attractive stubborn inner strength. Against reasonable judgement he opted to give Christie *yet another* chance. With Janni's blessing he drove out to Beaconsfield to observe her on-set work. To his great credit, by all accounts, even at this late state he still stalked her 'with an absolutely open mind.'

Everything conspired against Christie that crucial afternoon. Her scenes for the day had been gruelling and, though costumed and coiffured like a doll, she looked jaded – a fatal blend. Schlesinger is forthright: 'She had inches of make-up on and sported an unattractive hairstyle. She looked dreadful. She put me off.' It didn't help that an old chum of Schlesinger's, an actor of some repute working on *The Fast Lady,* roundly denounced her. She was, the actor insisted, 'hopeless' – fifty other pretty girls could do this, or Schlesinger's job, with double the style.

Forewarned and fully decided, Schlesinger backed off. He bade courteous adieu, drove back to Mayfair and told Janni he knew now who he wanted for Liz: a busty, vivacious girl with little more experience than Christie (but who had come good in the tests) called Topsy Jane. Janni accepted his young director's final word and the starting gun for *Billy Liar* was at last sounded. Less than a week later, the production – and elusive Lizzie – were in hot water. Topsy Jane fell ill and urgent replacement was sought.

Licking her wounds back in the bosom of her ragged, beloved Earl's Court flat, Christie knew nothing of the continuing real-life drama of *Billy Liar.* Already she was on the pay-phone to her agent, needling for further possible auditions, chances beyond Independent Artists. At the same time Schlesinger was agonizing, repeatedly rerunning the Julie Christie tests. 'We knew she was in *Crooks Anonymous* at the New Victoria,' he says, 'but we thought it best to skip that.' Against all obstacles, with considerable footage of *Billy Liar* already in the can, Christie suddenly had Schlesinger's blessing. There was, undeniably, very much a ring of 'second best' about the choice and Christie knew this; but she wasn't deterred and at first interpreted her reduced status as a challenge. As soon as she got Schlesinger's call – on the pay-phone at her flat – she was enthusing, unequivocally telling friends and acquaintances that she had landed her first really worthwhile part.

The Fast Lady, meanwhile, went on general release to indifferent notices but generally good audiences. Its main problem was its timing, swamped by a flood of similar, though less measured 'team' comedies. Though *The Times* charitably (and fairly) saw it as 'a potted history of British humour through the ages' most critics fixed attention on its fragile patina of stylistic quasi-Ealing comedy. In reality, the film was robust and substantial and embraced a huge range of comedy devices – from the parodying of quintessential English 'qualities', through the gentle subversion of Ealing's heyday, to unadulterated slapstick. Though Baxter was the star (in the sense that all the punchline comedy was generated through him), Annakin had refined his team-playing ideal – much in line with the *Carry On* and *Doctor* film approach. In this spirit, every biggish role was carefully sketched and cast.

Baxter played the moronic Murdoch Troon, foil to fellow lodger Freddy Fox (Leslie Phillips), an unctuous car salesman obsessed with women. Fox sells a clapped-out vintage Bentley, the Fast Lady of the title, to Troon, unwittingly winning for bug-eyed Troon the bug-eyed devotion of Claire Chingford (Christie), who happens to love old cars. Fox fancies Claire but is keen to acquire the agency for her father's (James Robertson Justice) motor business. Thus, he starts to fan the flames of the Troon-Claire *affaire,* on the promise that Troon will swing the agency deal for him. Troon is thereby exposed to the seemingly endless wrath of Claire's bumptious father and staggers from indignity to disaster in the cause of attempting to thaw him. Convinced that Troon is a halfwit, the father forbids Claire to see him again until he can prove himself by the simple expedient of passing a driving test. Unfortunately, in the middle of his vital test, Troon gets caught up in a bank robbery car chase. He fails his test – in a slick and well-staged lunatic chase reminiscent of the Keystone Cops – but gets the girl just the same. The story was, to be sure, peopled with stereotypes but the narrative enshrined the quirky charm that made Ealing comedies Britain's best fifties' export – and in gorgeous Eastman colour too. Christie, from the start, said she hated it, and in so doing effectively blocked negative personal notices. Hardly anyone mentioned her – though on screen she *looked,* at least, delectable. The *Monthly Film Bulletin* concentrated on the brash portrayal of current fads therein: 'the Twist, sentimental Scottish songs, vintage cars, the driving test, and an assortment of fashionable popsies' – of whom, presumably, Christie was cheerleader. Unforgivably, the *Bulletin* condemned a 'banal script . . . an attempt to please an affluent society.' Thirteen years earlier a similar criticism of principle might easily (equally unreasonably) have been launched against Ealing's *Passport to Pimlico* which addressed itself to nobler values perhaps, but in an identical way.

Amidst the flak, Leonard Mosley's devotion to Christie did not waver. In his merry review he pointedly concluded, just in case anyone missed it: 'The girl in the story is, by the way, the nuzzlesome newcomer named Julie Christie.' The *Express*, at any rate, was determined she wouldn't be lost in the mire. Contrary to her own beliefs, Annakin's films had helped her considerably – as had the reviled sexy pin-up sessions which she had sat for glamour magazines when cash was short. All around town now she bad-mouthed her past work. A colleague who occasionally drank with her at a Kensington pub recalls: 'She didn't want to know when the conversation turned that way. She was quite clear in her opinions of good and bad. From now on, she just wanted to do good things, big things. She was starry-eyed about Schlesinger . . . and the future.'

Christie's life during this period was a series of minor upheavals. Improving finances allowed her to move flat yet again, but she kept the varied sharing arrangement. She went to pubs but did not drink much. Often described as a beer-swilling extrovert, she in fact disliked beer and was usually uneasy amid new faces. Kevin McHugh, an Irish actor later to find celebrity at the Abbey Theatre, frequented a pub on the Fulham Road called the Queen's Elm and played darts with Christie's long-term boyfriend Don Bessant, who was only then arriving on the scene. McHugh remembers Christie a long time after *Billy Liar*: 'She was very quiet and proper and didn't play darts with the boys or anything like that. I remember her quietly sitting in a corner, sipping a drink. Well-behaved, polite, attractive. The Queen's Elm became a very popular theatrical and artists' meeting place in the late sixties and Julie and Bessant obviously liked the atmosphere – but there was nothing starry or brash about her . . . she was one of the lads.'

Christie had yet to settle into a relationship with Royal College of Art student Bessant when *Billy Liar* got underway. His arrival on the scene, many later said, helped shape her own thoughts about a future career. For now there was still mysterious confusion. Roderick Mann, the celebrated film journalist, remembers a revealing, immediately inexplicable incident. Now Hollywood-based and much admired for his integrity and discernment by stars and star-watchers alike, Mann was surprised one day to receive a call from Cary Grant. The subject of Grant's inquiry, from the other side of the world, was Julie Christie. Fresh from the heady success of Hitchcock's *North by Northwest,* Grant was widely diversifying again. Upcoming projects included the comedy *That Touch of Mink* and Stanley Donen's thriller *Charade.* Grant had seen a picture of Christie in a high-gloss magazine and wanted to get in touch with her. He was, he said, helping with casting on a movie and was keen on what he'd seen and read about Julie.

'I rang Julie Christie and passed on the phone message,' Mann later wrote in some dismay.

'Who wants me?' Christie queried flatly, coolly.
'Cary Grant.'
Mann wrote: 'It went down with a dull thud. The greatest name in showbusiness, the man hundreds of girls would crawl through a mortar barrage to meet – it meant nothing. I could as well have said: Mickey Hargitay. "OK," she said. "Thanks." She never did ring him.'
A close friend of Christie's told Mann: 'Julie's never really aware of the time or the date, or where she's put anything. She lives in a state of confusion. A chaotic girl.' More likely, in the case of Grant's interest, she was scared. More than once she confessed to intimates her wariness of America. 'At that stage,' says one, 'Hollywood played no realistic part in what she was doing.'
Michael Hayes elaborates: 'Her ambitions appeared to be to *get on* in theatre, and make good. Nothing avaricious or out-of-proportion.' Ultimately, initially, Hollywood was to live up to her fears. Her first stateside film trip, in 1965, she called 'horrible'. Grant's approach was also badly timed, coinciding as it did with her biggest rows with Independent and Schlesinger's interest. Grant personified sophisticated light cinema, the apparent American equivalent of Ken Annakin's ideal and, as everyone now knew, she wanted a clean break with that.
Billy Liar earned Christie £1,000, the London Film Critics' Guild award and altered the course of her life and career. In all she had less than two weeks' work on the movie – only eleven minutes of screen time in a film so spectacularly dominated by the wiry, winsome Courtenay. Still, she shone through, stunning critics and public alike. David Shipman, the film historian, wrote: 'Julie Christie's entrance in *Billy Liar* is one of the most beguiling things in sixties cinema: a long fugue in which she wanders gaily through the streets of a northern town, swinging a large handbag. The sequence owes something to the *nouvelle vague*, and as that was a liberating movement, so is she a liberating spirit.' On set in Bradford for a week she was timid, painfully conscious of the chance afforded her. Her nerves were bad and the initial excitement of netting the role was gone, to be replaced by a crushing depression. After Topsy Jane's bad luck it now felt, Christie reported, 'just like wearing someone else's clothes.' Schlesinger made it easy, talked to her, listened, encouraged. But he was after perfection, he demanded a quality performance. This minor character was the vibrant catalyst of the film, the girl who changes Billy's dreamy life – if only temporarily.
'I knew that the introduction of the girl was the key point,' Schlesinger said. 'Though I didn't then realize it would make such a big [career] change for her. The walk sequence was pieced together bit by bit. I'd had a long argument with the cameraman (Denys Coop) about the use of the cinemascopic zoom lens. He said it couldn't be

VENTILATOR

done in winter, in that light. He just wouldn't use that bloody zoom lens. So we shot rather unsatisfactorily in Bradford for a week. I wasn't satisfied . . . I didn't have the sequence I wanted. So we did a little bit more in London, when the weather was better.' The area Schlesinger and his location manager chose was around Tottenham Court Road, where a vast building reconstruction scheme was in progress, making the district look not unlike swelling Bradford. In the editing rooms Schlesinger assembled the bits and pieces from Bradford and London to create the famous 'walk sequence'. Before the film was halfway through he saw he had something – and someone – special at hand. 'It's easy to be wise after the event,' he says. 'But we watched her and said, "By God, we have a star!"'

For her part, Christie had no idea how good or bad she'd been. But the experience of gritty location work – so far removed from the sequined nonsense of Beaconsfield – rigidly decided her: she would not make another Annakin comedy, neither would she even contemplate a script in any way exploitive of her sexuality. 'I'd rather starve,' she told friends – this time with an ominous emphasis.

Even before *Billy Liar* reached the cinemas in September 1963 the first real dam-burst of script offers had started. Most, as expected, were light comedies and all were bluntly turned down. One projected script did pose problems though. Jack Davies, writer of *Crooks Anonymous* and *The Fast Lady*, was already at work on the third contracted film for Independent. Leslie Phillips recalls: 'It was to be set in France, something to do with a jolly journey through the continent. Julie was to be the girl, the glamour element – what else?' Producer Parkyn was keen to make the film but he was very aware of Christie's unease. On top of that, he was having distributor problems. Parkyn made no objection when Christie fled for a brief Mediterranean holiday then offered herself to rep work, finding easy placement in Birmingham in June.

'That summer was pretty chaotic,' says a publicist. 'There were problems between Rank, the distributors, and the Annakin producers. Julie owed them the picture but she hung back and the gods were on her side. After protracted hassles the producers wrapped up her contract and let her go on her way. That was the end of Julie and British comedy. She wanted to rebuild herself and she started out immediately. The papers were full of the story. They said she insisted on vetting all photos now, that she didn't want any more of that [the glamour] type. She was going to be a serious actress whether anyone liked it or not.'

Leslie Phillips saw the generosity of Parkyn and Wintle: 'Let's face it, they could have held her. But they were men of integrity and they'd learnt what she wanted and was capable of. When *Billy Liar* came along we were all envious. Sure, we said, that's the kind of picture

Previous page: With Tom Courtney in *Billy Liar*

we'd like to make. Julie just grabbed it with both hands and left. I can't say I got the chance to know her well. On those two movies we worked hard, long hours – longer than films today – and there wasn't much time for idle chit-chat. But I'd been with her long enough to admire her – just as the producers did. She was at heart a charming, lovely girl.'

The swing from Beaconsfield to Birmingham rep work took much courage, everyone agreed. Not only was the drop in earnings colossal but the precedents were not good. Many well-placed actors before her had chanced the backward step and never regained themselves. Christie had reason to worry.

A strong source of encouragement was 23-year-old Don Bessant, a rangy good-looking lithographer, a former postman, who was studying art and had gravitated towards Christie's indigent matey group in a casual way. (Legend has it that Bessant first met Christie when delivering a fan letter, and the attraction was immediate.) All her friends, in fact, approved of Birmingham. 'It was,' says Michael Hayes, 'something she had to do, an exercise, an extension of Central, an exorcism.'

Birmingham Repertory Theatre was a splendid oasis – a close-knit, spirited company that boasted respectable, highly-promising talents like Sheila Gish and Christopher Bidmead and had on its schedule some testing dramas. But Christie's initial dislike of the city – simply a side-effect of missing her London friends – darkened the early days. She was unexciting in the eleventh-billing part in Wycherley's *The Country Wife,* the first production that ran through June at the Station Street theatre, but found her feet quickly and progressed interestingly through *Thark* by Ben Travers, plays by Brecht, James Saunders and Anouilh. As she found the right digs 'with a dear, sweet landlady' and the London mates visited, she visibly relaxed and her performances improved yet more. Theatrical talent scouts were sent to see her and some, particularly those from the Royal Shakespeare Company down the road at Stratford, were particularly impressed. Still, there were disasters. In a revue by Malcolm Bradbury, Jim Duckett and David Lodge she sang a blues song alone on stage. Next day the local newspaper granted her the worst notice of her career: 'Julie Christie should never, ever, be allowed to sing unaccompanied on stage again.'

She never was allowed – and that suited her perfectly. The six-month Birmingham contract fortified the conviction that her best talent lay in 'straight' drama. But so far there were only admirers, no buyers. *Billy Liar* might just be a one-shot opportunity, destined to do well and die. In a year's time she might be grovelling for work.

By autumn, though she kept up a brave face, the riddle of the future had become a cause of some concern.

She was still in Birmingham, settled now, as much in love with the city as the work, when *Billy Liar* blazed onto the big screen. It was an instant box-office hit, a story of fantasy failings, a story for the times. Billy was a compulsive liar who rules non-existent Ambrosia while ambling through the mean streets of downtown Bradford. His dream is Capital Success but his world is immovably bounded by a grim job (in an undertakers') and a strict home life. Liz is the gypsy who prods him towards real escape – to the safe anonymity of London – but Billy never gets further than the local train station. 'Our first introduction to Liz,' said the *Monthly Film Bulletin,* 'is a bit of New Wave-style filmmaking which has been genuinely assimilated, and therefore genuinely works. One can't quite believe in her relationship with Billy, yet the unforced way the character is presented somehow makes her the most interesting person on the screen.' In *Sight and Sound* Peter Harcourt stamped radiant approval – both on Christie's style and Schlesinger's fussy perfectionism: 'Most remarkable and most unBritish is the zoom-tracking episode when Liz first comes to town . . . the camera follows her easily, observing her mugging response to everything she sees . . . Julie Christie as Liz gives, to my mind, the most stunningly attractive female performance that we've seen on the British screen.' And *The Times*, never easily moved towards superlatives, even conceded: 'She has that rare quality of obliterating everything else from the screen whenever she moves across.'

The tidal wave response, witnessed even at the early previews, apparently failed to touch Christie. In truth, she was probably stunned – surprised beyond all expectation – numb. From her Birmingham bedsit at Forest Road, Moseley, she greeted the first flocks of revived journalists calmly. She told the *Evening Standard*: 'When I finish working here at Christmas I have nothing to to. I would like to find more stage work. But if nothing turns up I will go to Greece for a bit. . .' She still missed her London friends (the real reason why she couldn't continue at Birmingham), but had no plans for settling down, let alone marriage. She laughed off the notion of herself as an 'established actress' and suggested her main concern was learning the ropes. In London she would seek a grander flat, near Olympia – to be shared once again 'with a group of good friends' – and there she would base her future career efforts. She could not afford to buy a flat – 'I'm earning £16 a week in rep!' – but wasn't troubled by income. She had only once chatted with the man her agent described as her accountant and estimated her savings were negligible anyway.

But she was happy, happier than she had been since those early overworked student days at Central. She wore no make-up and her clothes 'appeared to have been put through the wringer, dry'. Gone was the pomp and pretence of Beaconsfield – to be replaced by the quiet enthusiasm fired by half-promises from scene-setters like Schlesinger. Already he had been on the phone to her, congratulating,

At Birmingham rep in *The Country Wife. Left to right:* Christopher Bidmead, William Ingram, Sheila Gish, Julie Christie

sketching future possibilities.

While the *Evening Standard* man speculated on the next tricky steps to real stardom Julie mused along obligingly, not particularly committed. The most hopeful project awaiting her, it was agreed, was John Schlesinger's planned new wave film 'about the rich and gilded kitchen sinks'. Julie didn't seem bothered either way. 'I *think* I'm to be the leading lady,' she shrugged. 'I don't know for sure. No one tells me anything except chauffeurs and people. I think we shall shoot it in Brighton and I'll be a poor girl who becomes rich and miserable.'

According to the *Standard,* she was laughing when she made the prediction. *Darling,* the rich-little-poor-girl story, Schlesinger's personal reward for *Billy Liar,* was already in screenplay preparation.

TEMPORARY FREEDOM

The conflict and contradictions remained. Here she was, twenty-two – already a star risen, and set, and risen again – hiding away in the sticks, unhappy whenever she saw herself in a newspaper, unhappier still when she looked in a mirror. And yet, she was full of the courage of leaving home comforts behind, full of energy, and amorphous ambitions. Looking back on her first encounters with Schlesinger she told friends, 'I was frightened of John . . . but I was frightened of everyone then.'

Peter Evans, the showbiz writer, met her when she drove down from Birmingham to attend a *Billy Liar* showing and discovered a personality both rigid and brittle. Shortly before a London producer had grumbled to him: 'She's loaded with talent . . . If only she would behave like a star.' At lunch with Evans she kicked off her shoes and curled her feet under her. She was shy but straightforward, and she laughed a lot. Evans found 'this very quality, this oddball audacity . . . gives her the cutting edge on her perhaps more beautiful and more dignified rivals.'

She was, he judged, uneasy in the conventional film star role because 'she is too much woman, too spirited to be tied and stamped'. If, as she claimed, she was intimidated by top-rank journalists like Evans, she covered-up well enough. With challenging directness she told him: 'I don't move around in a chi-chi crowd or anything and when I've got a bit of cash I'm inclined to spread it round.' Comparison with other star British actresses was dismissed. 'I read about people like Samantha Eggar and Sarah Miles talking about property they're buying and real estate and everything . . . of course they've got their heads screwed on the right way and are terribly ambitious about the future. But I'm not like that. I mean, everything that happens to me is a terrible surprise. The future for me doesn't exist. And I love my freedom.'

In *Young Cassidy* which director John Ford was unable to complete. Jack Cardiff finished the picture

The fact that *Billy Liar* had already attracted unified ear-splitting praise – and the implications in terms of her renewed star exposure – she tried to ignore. But finally, and to Evans, she confessed, 'I'm so scared of what *Billy Liar* could lead to . . . it's almost like a trap really. At the moment I have the guts to turn down film roles because I want to stay in rep for a while. But . . . if the offers get better and bigger and the pressure is put on – what then?' There was no way, she stressed, she wanted to get caught on the roundabout of image-making again – 'worrying about my dark roots showing through and whether my nails need another coat of varnish'. Birmingham wasn't so bad, she told Evans. 'And if this little lot doesn't work out, I still have my air-mattress.'

But *Billy* had worked out and the pressures she was loath to acknowledge were building furiously. Jo Janni waited till the film was cut and released before he summoned her and proposed a contract. In Janni's maverick style, the contract was unorthodox. He would, he suggested, retain her services for four years, during which time she would appear in whatever film projects he launched *or* personally chose for her; for this, in the old-world American studios fashion, he would pay her a regular yearly salary; on her earnings for additional films outside his corral she would pay him a clear fifty per cent. Janni was a charming, plain-speaking man and Christie found his unadorned approach (and the evidence of *Billy Liar*) vastly reassuring.

Persuasive too was a project he was hatching called *Darling* which, he assured her, Schlesinger intended to compose especially for her, with ace screenwriter Frederic Raphael. Though he could make no positive promises about her casting, *Darling* would, he swore, appease her sensibilities. It would be something special . . . all provided that everything slotted into place and the movie got off the ground. Christie was realistic enough to appreciate the facts as Janni stated them: the financing of a big movie often depends on casting an established lead; all Janni could promise was his very best efforts to secure her as a lead – in *Darling* and other major works. After talks with her agents, Christie quickly decided to abandon her well-voiced resolve and sign yet another film contract.

But before bowing into Janni's camp there was time for one last burst of freedom. The talent scouts of the Royal Shakespeare Company who had admired Christie on stage in Birmingham now shuffled up an offer. At Christmas, along with fellow rep member Elisabeth Spriggs, she was signed for a five-month run of *A Comedy of Errors,* due to be taken on world tour to mark the four hundredth anniversary of Shakespeare's birth. The director was Stratford veteran Peter Brook, fresh from his own movie success with *Lord of the Flies* (1962). When the signing was announced on January 8th Christie declared herself 'absolutely thrilled'; she had, she said, always cherished secret ambitions to appear in Shakespeare. That, true enough, was half the story; but she was also ecstatic at the thoughts of four months travelling through Europe and America, living out of a suitcase, never stopping anywhere long enough to be lonely. For a while too she would be away from agents and moguls and promises and pressures.

A Comedy of Errors rehearsed at Stratford then ran for eleven lukewarm performances at London's Aldwych Theatre between January 21st and February 8th. Immediately after, the 55-member company headed off on the European leg of its tour, the play being performed side-by-side with *King Lear* which featured Paul Scofield in the lead. In West Berlin on the tour's first stop, on February 17th, *King Lear* stole the evening. There were fifteen curtain calls before Scofield and director Brook were obliged to beg the still-applauding audience: 'Please go home, it is late for us all.'

A Comedy of Errors, which numbered Diana Rigg, Alec McCowen and Ian Richardson among its 23-member cast, fared less well. The play was a reworking of the 1962 Stratford production which had then won good notices, but something was lacking this time out. Christie, one observer remarked, seemed 'tipsily impressed' by her role. She played Luciana, the slightly-delineated sister of Adriana who confuses Antipholus of Syracuse with Adriana's husband and displays some distress when he starts making advances to her. She presumably marries Antipholus after the errors have been resolved at the end – but her function is not greatly interesting and only a very exceptional stage actress could make the part memorable.

To her considerable anguish, Christie learnt here that she was not an exceptional stage actress. *Newsweek* charitably summed up the production's short American stay: 'To say that no one noticed her would be a base canard. A pretty girl on stage can never go unnoticed.' But nobody had much else to say about her, or her lacklustre performance. Only two of New York's daily newspaper critics cited her by name and then it was only to say how decorative she appeared. Paul Scofield perceptively observed her struggle to come to terms with her weak stage presence: 'She is not yet secure on the stage,' he said. 'But this inexperience doesn't come across on the screen. She has a genuine talent. I admire her enormously on screen.'

To be fair, it seems Christie herself foresaw problems in matching RSC standards when she took the part of Luciana. Though she told writer Tony Crawley at the time that she 'loved the experience . . . I'd go back on stage any time . . . just get me something good to do', she later revealed herself to friends and journalists. The Shakespearian playing was self-exploration, testing her real capacities after the heady rush of *Billy Liar.* In 1983 she accepted journalist Andrew Duncan's suggestion that the RSC 'reinforced her feelings that she was too nervous to be a good stage actress'.

The tour itinerary meanwhile was a source of consolation. West Berlin, Prague, Budapest, Belgrade, Bucharest, Warsaw, Helsinki, Leningrad, Moscow . . . Christie drank in the sights and sounds, took time whenever she could to go out on the streets and amble about, gypsying. Leningrad she enjoyed, Moscow was awe-inspiring, slightly shocking. 'We went directly from Moscow to New York,' she said later, recalling the memorable moments. 'At first the contrast was awful. I had been struck by the authority and discipline in Moscow and New York was the complete opposite. But I liked it very, very much.'

During almost two months in America, *A Comedy of Errors* played Washington, Boston, Philadelphia and New York, running longest in the last venue. Christie relaxed best in New York, though her ambivalent reactions suggest she was not unhappy when the play ended. She hung out with new chums in Greenwich Village where she found 'a lot of trash going on . . . but at least there are people trying to do things. Half of them are phony and terribly bad, but there's so much vitality.' Once again it was the impoverished artists who impressed her – the painters and buskers and pocketbook philosophers just in the process of shifting affinities from Kerouac to Ken Kesey. But she liked the pure fun too: 'I went to so many places and actually heard and saw the musicians I'd only heard on record before – people like Sonny Rollins. I'm mad about modern jazz music and I love to dance. . .'

While the travels and fresh experiences relieved her anxieties, back home a formidable array of big name filmmakers was hunting her services. Charlton Heston, negotiating the $3.8 million production *The War Lord* with Universal, arranged a special screening of *Billy Liar* and decided she was perfect for his co-lead – a decision of major significance as she had not yet won any attention in America. In his diary he wrote 'She has a natural quality, she's very striking and she can act.'

The suggestion was duly made to Universal and formal negotiations with Christie's agents began. Christie's asking price, judging on the script, was a not-too-expensive $35,000 which to Heston seemed reasonable. But Universal took a different stance, assessing her a minor actress. 'We tried very hard to get her,' says Heston, 'and we could have – for thirty-five thousand. Since she was shortly to become an international star of considerable importance, this would have been a bargain. But the studio balked at what they felt was the excessive price.' *The War Lord* deal collapsed and Christie, in Europe, was informed by telephone. She reacted with the same inspired indifference she'd adopted to talk of *Darling*.

Around the same time an even brighter film luminary, the legendary John Ford, sent his script for *Young Cassidy* along. As in *Billy Liar*, the role on offer was brash and tarty – and small. When Christie's

A studio shot from *Young Cassidy*

agent phoned with the news Julie was more enthusiastic. Ford was the best of directors, a man of integrity, a man tuned to his faithful international audience – a model of excellence for anyone keen on a future in wide-appeal movies. Fees were never a contentious issue. Christie relished the opportunity of the international break and urged the settlement of the deal.

As her months of travel drew to a close she could reflect on a period that was problematic but greatly refreshing. She had indulged herself in many delightful ways – she had seen a lot of art and antiques and had read omniverously. She had dashed through *Lolita, Alice in Wonderland,* countless quality novels. Victoriana interested her and she devoured books on related subjects – biographies, social studies, everything. In Europe and New York she had found time to root out odd antique items, fascinatingly attractive junk like the old coffee grinder she lovingly cradled in her arms through customs at Heathrow, the pride of her catches. Her recently cultivated interest in impressionism was fuelled by trips to art galleries everywhere. Gaugin and Matisse were her special favourites but the Russian art she had seen in Leningrad had enthralled her, won her forever.

Unquestionably, the RSC tour had been a growing-up time. And yet, many associates suggest, there was still an underlying immaturity. One colleague says: 'After all, she was – what? – twenty-three, twenty-four. She'd had no marvellous education and much of her time was spent script-reading as opposed to anything else.' He hurries to emphasise: 'One thing she wasn't was pretentious. If she bored you with art details, or whatever, she wasn't trying to impress. You must remember the press had been hounding her for years already. So she had to come up with answers. So when they said, Who are your favourite actors? She'd say Brando, Maggie Smith. But those were in a sense answers she *had to* give. She was very young. Did she know what or who she *really* liked? I think like most young people she was in a state of constant change – especially young people under such extreme pressures.'

By the time the RSC tour was winding down in America Janni and Schlesinger's preparation for *Darling* was far advanced. As Janni supposed, there had been difficulties raising finance. First approaches to every major company met with blank responses. 'They said I must be mad,' Janni groaned. 'Wanting £400,000 with an unkown girl as a star. You can have your money, they said, if you use Shirley MacLaine or someone like that.' Eventually a tentative financing structure was arranged, fully dependent on securing a sound star name for the lead male role. To that end, Schlesinger flew to New York to court the megastars. Everyone admired Frederic Raphael's blisteringly original script, but its uncompromising boldness – years ahead of its time – turned the cautious away. Paul Newman rejected the lead role,

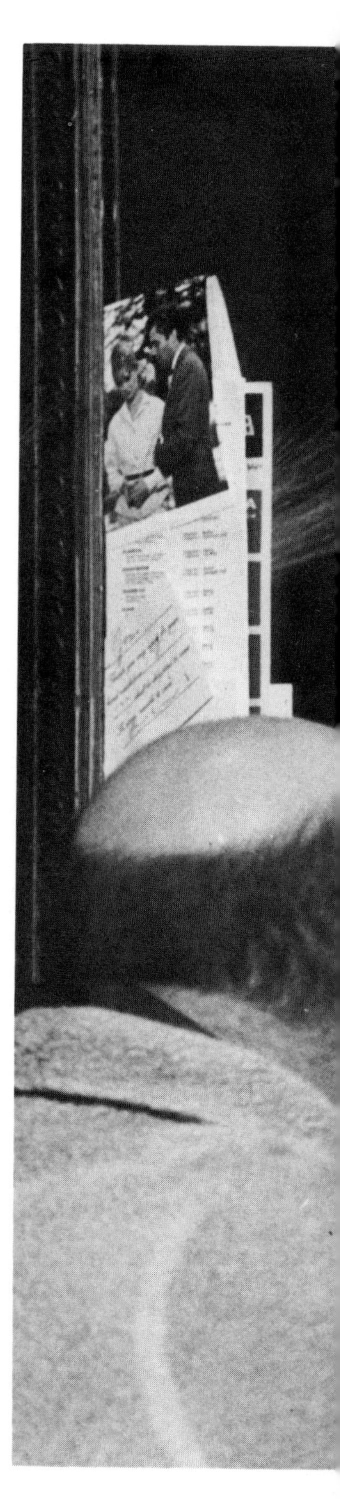

Gregory Peck followed, even the adventurous Cliff Robertson.

Schlesinger pretended not to hear the portents of doom. Instead he 'prepped' himself with Christie, visiting her in Philadelphia and sitting long into the night at her hotel, poring over Raphael's lines. He declined the offer to attend her RSC show because, 'For one thing I gathered she was not brilliant in it and for another she was playing the same part my sister had played at Stratford, and she had died recently.' All energies were fixed on priming her for her huge and complicated *Darling* role instead.

Christie, for her part, was a little confused by the complex Diana of the script, a greedy trollop who brings about her own tragic downfall. Later she told Tony Crawley: 'I never thought I could play the part anyway, I was embarrassed by the whole thing . . . The script went through a lot of story changes . . . I wasn't terribly interested. Just write it down, I'd say. I just didn't have a lot of confidence then.' Schlesinger had yet to make his mind up about Christie's preparedness – though, whichever way, he was determined, on instinct, after their chemistry on *Billy Liar* – to cast her. He flew back to Britain, less sure than ever of the financial solidity of the project, and offered the male lead to Dirk Bogarde. In his autobiographical volume *Snakes and Ladders,* Bogarde recalled Schlesinger's frank admission:

'This is not going to be a prestige picture. By that I mean there is no money, and really no one wants to make it except me and the girl and Jo Janni.'

'Who is the girl?' Bogarde asked.

'Oh, you wouldn't know her, just starting; brilliant – that's been the problem. We can't find a man to play the second role.'

'But who is the girl?'

'Called Julie Christie. She's marvellous; huge future.'

Bogarde, in fact, did know her, had seen her in *Andromeda* – 'that space fiction thing'. He told Schlesinger: 'I'll do it. I want to work with you and I want to work with Christie . . . She's The Young. I want to be with the young.'

Schlesinger's pernickety insistence on seeing things right almost caused a last-minute hitch. He wanted to screen test the well-experienced Bogarde – to make sure he wouldn't be, as the director feared, 'too *soigné*'. Finally, graciously, Bogarde agreed, the tests looked good and new investors were sought. Within a month a reluctant deal was made. The National Film Finance Corporation and distributors Anglo-Amalgamated put up a hefty chunk of cash, strengthened by 'every penny Janni had to his own name'.

And so, with a ramshackle finance structure, an actress fresh from an undistinguished part and last-chance supporting players, *Darling* lurched haltingly into preproduction. Janni's shirt was on it, as was Schlesinger's still delicate reputation. But all eyes were on Julie

Previous page: A pensive John Schlesinger on the set of *Darling*

Christie. All around Wardour Street – even beyond, in America now – everyone waited and watched and wondered could she distinguish herself in lead part playing.

There were moments of minor triumph and excitement in the calm before the storm of *Darling*. *A Comedy of Errors* found its happiest audience on June 18th in a special performance for the Queen at Windsor Castle, where Christie crushed her nerves and presented a fine Luciana. It was the first time legitimate actors had trod the castle boards in fifty years and the Queen, according to the London *Daily Mail* 'loved the comedy. She shook with laughter and more than once had to wipe tears of laughter from her eyes.' This triumph at the end of a rocky run absolved everyone.

Don Bessant, Christie's artist boyfriend, grew closer, more supportive, and they openly talked of their love. Back in London Christie and Bessant – together with painter mate Alfie Benge – took a new flat, part of an Edwardian block situated between Earl's Court and Hammersmith, and filled their free time with forays through the antique markets of Portobello Road, searching out oddball furnishings. Their first acquisition, draped with a mixture of patriotism and irony in the dingy hallway, was a huge pop-art Union Jack. But ideas for furnishings were more abundant than the cash to acquire them. For a long time the flat reflected her previous, more flea-bitten abodes: lots of piled-up, half-read books, the work of her artist mates crammed onto every wall, cheap carpets and curtains.

Questioned about possible marriage to Bessant – which most casual acquaintances expected at some stage – Christie just hedged: 'Marriage is such a serious thing, such a difficult thing. It requires a particular talent, like writing, like acting . . . and I haven't got it. Marriage is becoming increasingly incompatible with modern living. But if you find someone you love what else is there to do except live with them and take no notice of what people say? Love is the most important thing to a woman . . . to me, at least.'

In this same long interview, with Oriana Fallaci, Christie made stammery declarations she would, in later years, vehemently reverse. With the blundering uncertainty of the time she stated: 'Man is a more intelligent animal. Why? – I don't know. Maybe for a woman, using her brain is not the most important thing.' She also acknowledged the importance of long-term fidelity and motherhood: 'Sometimes, yes, I feel the need for a child.' Almost twenty years later, still marriage-free, still nervously inarticulate (by her own judgement) but firmly feminist she would say: 'The reason women think about getting older is that they've been taught by men to believe they're no longer attractive then. At the root of it all is that you don't exist in the eyes of the male population, but there are fifty percent of your own type you can appeal to. It's a thoughtless presumption that if you don't get a man to stand by you for the rest of your life you don't exist.' At forty-three the notion of child-bearing was less agreeable too: 'Do I want to spend the latter part of my life with a growing-up child, poor sod?'

Those considerations, in the summer of '64, were breezier, more optimistic. The few short weeks' work on John Ford's film, *Young Cassidy,* based in Ireland, were nerve-making but happy. Christie's sequences as prostitute Daisy Battles who seduces young playwright Cassidy (Rod Taylor) were among the first to be shot. When Ford arrived in Ireland he was ailing, frail in movement and almost blind. He was sixty-eight, veteran of 125 movies, the milestones of his cinematic achievements already far behind. But he approached *Young Cassidy* with the kind of fervid native-Irish keenness; the kind some said had weakened his objectivity and soured the comedic success of *The Quiet Man* (1952), his beloved paean to old Ireland, starring John Wayne and Maureen O'Hara.

Ford, whose real name was Sean O'Feeney, had long wanted to film the life of controversial Irish writer Sean O'Casey and had chosen one of O'Casey's autobiographical works, *Mirror in My House* – in itself a flawed, over-indulgent work – as the basis for a screen plotline. Sean Connery had rejected an offer to star but a host of others were ready to overlook story deficiencies for a chance to take the Master's direction. Christie, unashamedly, ranked with the latter. She looked forward to meeting Ford – who charmed her in his gentle, absent-minded way, as he charmed everyone.

But halfway through their scenes he fell ill and withdrew from the film. Cinematographer Jack Cardiff, only recently turned director, was swiftly summoned to fill the gap. Christie was disappointed and confused. For Cardiff, the process of assuming command in mid-shoot was chaotic and stressful, but he liked Christie and gave as much time and support as he could. 'Neither of us knew what I was supposed to do,' Christie says. The screenplay was compact and well-constructed but Cardiff could only speculate on Ford's intentions for characterizations. At the start, it seems, Cardiff was helped as much by Christie (who at least had discussed her role with Ford at some length) as she was by him. For a while Christie panicked: 'I thought: this is the end of my career.' But later, when she saw the final assemblage, she was surprised. 'My God, Christie,' she said to herself, 'you've come out of that very well. You even look beautiful!'

The popular press, eager to revamp the pin-up image of a year before, might have easily agreed but, surprisingly, hardly anyone took notice of her.

Her retreat to theatre had undoubtedly served to lessen public interest – a little more perhaps that Christie's agents cared to observe.

With Rod Taylor in *The Young Cassidy*, 1964

The Guardian, like most film reviews, saw no cause to mention her. *Young Cassidy* was for them 'not so much a film as a plethora of paradoxes'. In particular reviewer Richard Roud disdained the blotchy botched colour, the senseless evasion of major political events in Ireland at the time of the story (1910 to 1920) and the fact that never once is the film's hero, Cassidy, explained to be Sean O'Casey. 'All this apart,' Roud concluded, '*Young Cassidy* is not so bad.' The redoubtable *Monthly Film Bulletin*, however, was scathing: 'It has virtually no style or personality attributable to either Ford or Cardiff. What should have been vibrant, hard-hitting and redolent of its author's world becomes instead an anonymous work, weighed down by that feeling common to many British films of a script being faithfully shot page by page without any real creative participation from the director.' In the circumstances, the *Film Bulletin* might have been kinder and, with hindsight, the film seems, as the *Guardian* allowed, not so bad.

Offset with Rod Taylor on *Young Cassidy*

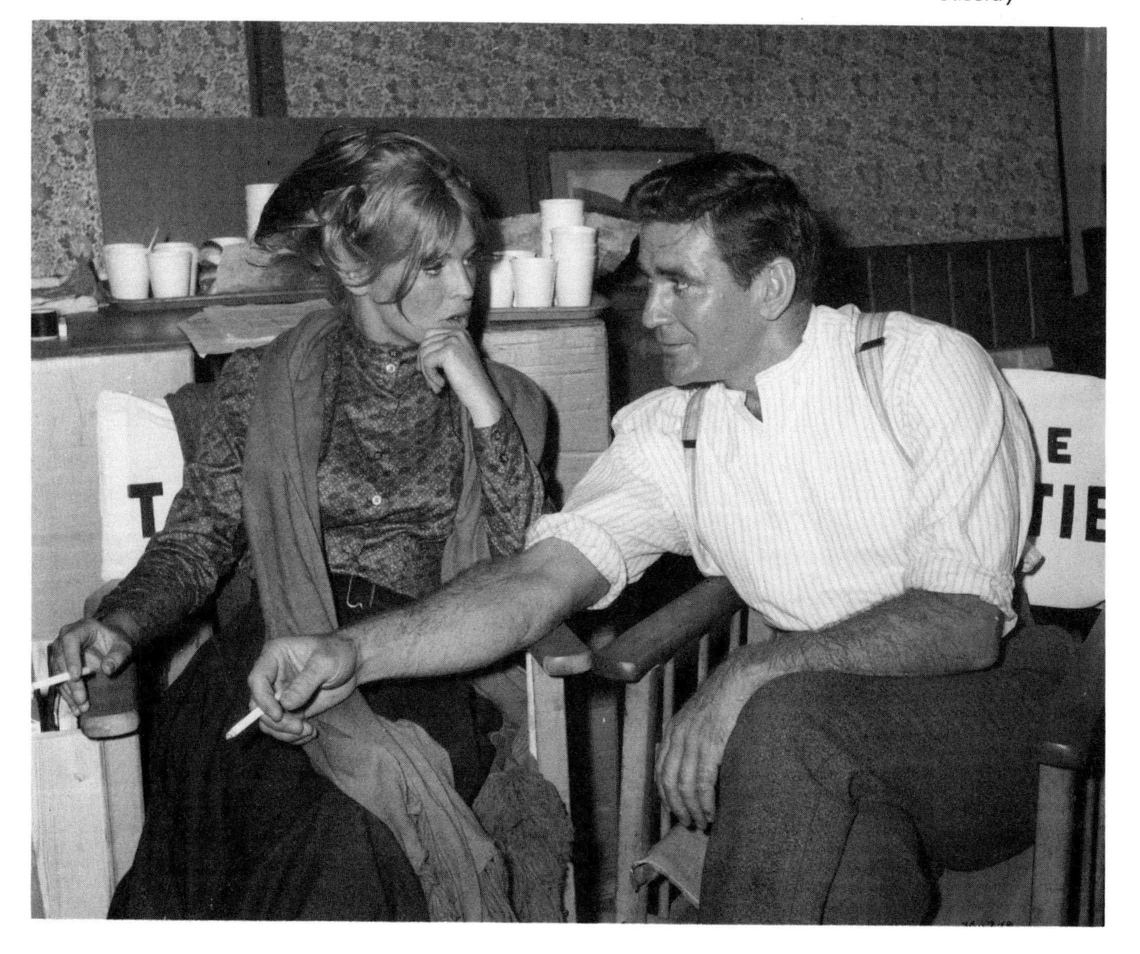

Cassidy-O'Casey, an impoverished idealist whose ambitions are restricted by the demands of looking after his family, journeys through the social injustices of Dublin life – involving himself with the rowdy tramwaymen strike, dawdling with prostitute Daisy, seeking a better life. He falls in love with bookshop assistant Nora (Maggie Smith) who encourages him towards a life of writing. Finding success at the Abbey Theatre, his unorthodox views estrange him from family friends and his own past. Unable to cope, Nora deserts him and he heads off for England alone. The narrative is pot-holed and unsatisfactory but the central performances rise to the challenge and everyone – Taylor, Smith, Michael Redgrave, Christie – discharge themselves honourably. Christie exudes sexuality but her lines are brief and the character might reasonably be seen as no more than an imaginative extension of *Billy Liar*'s Liz.

Still, the experience was edifying – not just because of those precious moments under Ford's direction, but she had seen too, at close-hand, the rigours of keeping a troubled production afloat. For the first time, she had truly, maturely *watched* the film-making process and assimilated the actor's part. Months earlier, on his first meeting her in Janni's office, screenwriter Frederic Raphael, then beavering away at an early draft of *Darling,* had noted: 'She was not very interested in our labours.' But now was different. Now she had some perspective. Theatre was not for her, the sexy posturing of her late teens had outlived its purpose and, blessedly, died. Similarly, bit parts in prestige movies were insufficient. She had eleven minutes in *Billy Liar,* little more in *Young Cassidy*. Bessant was ambitious for her and she found herself, suddenly, craving wider, more sure-footed acclaim. She was ready for Schlesinger and he, in his urge to consolidate his own lofty position in new wave cinema, was readier than ever for her.

'Christie's lovely walks to beautiful music were over,' *Newsweek* later recounted. 'The time was at hand for rigid discipline.'

At Shepperton Studios *Darling* was ready to roll. Julie's character, Diana, featured on every page of a fat, jam-packed script. It would be, for the first time, *her* film. All hers.

TESTING TRILBY

Julie Christie is the first to admit to the transformation that occurred with the making of *Darling*. Primarily it was, of course, the career gear-change that accelerated her into international stardom. More importantly in her eyes, it altered her personality. In the summer, attending an important premiere in London, her nerves had been so bad that she collapsed, missed the subsequent reception and was tended to by Sarah Miles, a stranger till then. Lack of readiness for the pressures of the business she denied. Instead, with ruthless self-honesty, she judged herself 'neurotic and inferior'. One of the greatest joys of the RSC tour had been the sense of escape, the anonymity of Eastern Europe and the States where, apart from the attention-draw of a curt 'New Faces' column in *Time,* she was unknown. That brief respite from the film business had been 'as exciting as a trip to the moon'.

But the return to London meant the reality of the contract with Janni and Schlesinger's unmatchable gusto. His determination to make *Darling* an earth-shaker terrified her in the beginning, but she learned to live with it. Her own freshening ambitions suppressed her nerves and by the time the three-and-a-half month production was finished she had quite changed. Months later she remarked, 'I might have been nicer before – but I've got more confidence now. I've quietened down.' Many aspects of the change were superficial and short-lived. But the hard-shell exterior that emerged, the response to real fame, was an irreversible development that was to grow and grow. Never again would the granting of interviews be casually undertaken. Rarely would she allow any public insights on her life and thoughts. *Darling* made Julie Christie and minted an enduring enigma.

Filming began in an atmosphere of stripped nerves and honest arguments. From Day One Schlesinger and Christie were at war – clear evidence perhaps that they fully understood the magnitude of

Darling

what they were trying. The script was still under revision and Christie was, more than once, called on to improvise her lead role – something she adjusted to like an old dab. But Schlesinger's intensity, she felt, was insane. The six o'clock calls at Earl's Court every morning were acceptable, but six- sometimes seven-day working weeks stretched her to breaking point. She cried a lot on set, was often unmanageably moody – then, like a cat, fell asleep for hours on end, a tactic she apparently frequently reverted to when unhappy. More than once schedules ran late when wardrobe and make-up were obliged to revive and re-dress a snoozing lead.

Though her deepening trust and affection for Schlesinger were obvious she bitterly complained, 'He goes potty . . . He goes on and on. I don't think he would ever sleep if he had his way. I don't mind hard work. I don't even mind just one day off a week. Or even one day a fortnight. But he's like an engine when he gets going.'

Schlesinger was philosophical when interviewed. He denied any friction but admitted 'once or twice we had a bad day'. With fatherly understanding he added: 'She needed an enormous amount of stamina for the part. Nevertheless, it was the best part written for any girl in British films in the last decade . . . I knew she was tired but I also knew there was no point being sympathetic. I was tired too, for that matter.'

Tiredness wasn't Schlesinger's only worry. Almost daily there came the anxious reports on the financial situation, that Janni's backers were every bit as reluctant as had been first supposed. Dirk Bogarde recalls a viewing of rushes after the first week's shooting. For him, till then, *Darling* was a happy film, in spite of all the creative jostling. Christie he adored, found her bubbly good company – in his words 'glorious, a gift'. But the backers were less compliant. The story of *Darling* they reckoned, quite reasonably, was a risky exposé of the squalor beneath the high gloss of the Swinging Sixties; it might not take much to nudge it over the edge of propriety into the realm of offensive trash. From an edgy, hypercritical viewpoint they watched the first footage of Christie. Bogarde remembers the initial reaction.

One said: 'She's got a face like the back of a bus. She looks just like a fella. Look at that jaw: she could play bloody football.'

Bogarde's friend and agent Tony Forwood quickly countered: 'I think she's the nearest thing I've seen to Brigitte Bardot.'

'You think she's *sexy*?' the incredulous investor barked.

'Very,' Forwood urged. 'She'll be a big, big star.'

Somewhat mollified by such emphatic assurance from an established, much admired star-watcher, the worried executives backed off. 'You heard what the gentleman said,' the top man sighed. 'Sexy? I must be losing my wits. It's all going mad. . .'

In mid-production a serious cash problem did almost scotch the film. Bogarde, on equal billing and salary with co-star Laurence Harvey,

With John Schlesinger during the shooting of *Darling*, 1965

was first to hear of it. Janni rushed to his dressing-room after a day's shoot. His face was pale as putty, according to Bogarde, and his eyes were hooped with fatigue.

'Disaster,' he told the actor. 'I've mortgaged everything; car, flat, stocks and shares, everything except Stella, my wife. Can you help us? Will you accept a cut in salary and defer you deferments?' Bogarde blithely consented, so pleased was he in the quality of purpose, and the film rolled jerkily forward.

Meawhile Christie worked, and slept. Laurence Harvey found her odd but engaging. 'She was always asleep,' he said. 'Coming to the studio in the morning, going home in the evening. She may even have been asleep while she was doing the picture . . . But she is marvellous, absolutely adorable, enchanting. . .'

Christie's semi-permanent – and real – exhaustion is excusable. Fourteen-hour working days alternated with rushed spells of housekeeping. After shooting every evening she taxied (or begged a lift) home to the flat in central London and made the beds and cooked for her still-penniless mates. Schlesinger was unaware of this till, in the trough of a particular row, while she was fighting a heavy-lidded torpor that hampered her performance, she admitted that she hadn't been to bed till one a.m.

Schlesinger was furious. 'I told her she had no right to [stay up so late]. But she explained she had to cook and clean her flat.' Chastened, Schlesinger consulted with Janni and back-up arrangements were made. Janni's Italian maid was despatched to help at the flat and Schlesinger's chauffeur was laid on. Performances improved, but Julie still snatched forty winks every forty minutes. Much of the reason for her frequent excessive exhaustion, friends suggest, was her stubborn refusal to adjust her home life to the demands of the shooting schedule. Among her own social group she was still the idle, heel-kicking nonconformist, burrowing in ancient cookbooks for obscure Victorian recipes, debating apt and meaningless philosophical issues, chain-smoking cigarettes till dawn.

'I doubt if she believed in *Darling*,' one colleague told me. 'Not in any total, important way. She had no notion of the riches and change it would bring her. She wanted to enjoy what she had, to keep on hanging round the boys, lazing, doing what she always did.' Dirk Bogarde observed what was, in his well-experienced eyes, a refreshing variation on the normal star temperament and character. Christie's behaviour was often more akin to the set-sweeper's indifference than the self-importance of key players. She dressed with a casualness that some might find unflattering.

Her hair was always awry, her hands unmanicured. In her bulging ragged old handgrip she carried spare sweaters, books, apples. Bogarde deeply sympathized with her problem of tiredness. One

With Dirk Bogarde

morning in particular, he recalls, on location at Paddington Station, she could barely stand up with sleepiness. When he queried her she told him that during the night the lilo air-mattress she was using (still!) had sprung a leak. She had slept as best she could on the bare floor, tossing and turning amid a tribe of adopted stray cats. But she wasn't despairing: she had just seen a proper bed that took her fancy – 'a brass antique with bobbles and bars, in a junk shop in the King's Road'. In the meantime patchwork repair to the lilo was necessary and she asked one of the film crew to fetch her some puncture-fix from a nearby garage. Bogarde writes in his autobiography:

'While she went off to have a pee in the Ladies, Forwood wrote out a modest cheque for the bedstead, and I did one for the mattress with a little left over for blankets, always supposing that she needed them. Which seemed more than possible. We put them in her handgrip and she was suprised to find them rummaging through later for an apple. . .'

Her engaging ingenuousness made Bogarde smile. The response to his gesture was typically guileless, without falsity of any kind.

'What's this for then?'

'For the bed and the mattress.'

She just smiled and bit her apple. 'Ta.' She needed the proper bed, had insufficient money still and was truly grateful for the star's generosity. The bed was purchased, and nothing more was said about it.

About halfway through the shoot, when the rushes had begun to look more promising and the backers less nervous, a difficult hurdle for Christie loomed. She had known for weeks the embarrassment that confronted her but had slyly ignored it, hoping Schlesinger would let it pass. As the darling of the title, Christie was Diana Scott, an unscrupulously ambitious model whose empty character mirrored the tinsel world of sixties' chic. Determined to advance her career at any cost, she manipulates a series of men, falling in love with one (Bogarde) by whom she becomes pregnant. She aborts the baby lest it interferes with her work, takes up with the mean and equally manipulative Miles Brand (Laurence Harvey) and loses Bogarde when she gets drawn into a life of sexual high jinks. After decadent adventures she opts for retirement and marriage with Prince Cesare della Romita (Jose-Luis de Vilallonga), residing with him in strained splendour at his Florentine palace. Finally, seeing the wastefulness of her life, she strips off the uniform of wealth – literally a strip scene – quits Italy and flies back to Bogarde to attempt, unsuccessfully, a fresh start.

The crucial scene, the ritual disrobing as she saunters through the vacant, chilly palace, Schlesinger and screenwriter Raphael painstakingly choreographed. It was, they believed, a profound moment, central to the theme: an unambiguous depiction of naked, imperfect reality that contrasts the dazzling razzmatazz of Diana's life. But by the time the filming of the sequence drew near, Christie was fairly drained from long arduous weeks and mentally at her lowest ebb. She decided, bluntly, that she did not want to strip for the cameras. For a start, she had begun to detest the character of Diana. 'Imagine living ten years of a woman's life in a few weeks,' she would grouse to friends, 'living every damned emotion!' Secondly, emphatically, she thought her nude body unattractive. Tensions mounted and the short, breathless rows with Schlesinger lengthened. She cried a lot, became distinctly awkward on set.

Schlesinger remembers: 'Here was a woman (Diana) who had wealth, everything; and she had to strip to symbolize the lonely naked creature underneath. It was a scene that demanded great acting, specially when she moved through six rooms and the camera tracked her through. But she would burst into tears at the mention of it. Whenever the costume had to be fitted she would make some excuse and stand like a sack of potatoes. She behaved like a dreadfully spoilt child, putting on a petulant act. I got really angry and decided she needed a bomb . . . and I gave it to her.' To Schlesinger's mind Christie 'knew this part was vital for her career' but that awareness and her commitment to him came unstuck now. After much dithering she cornered him and explained her fears about her 'very unattractive body'. The frank confession Schlesinger found surprising and endearing. He recounts: 'I told her, this nude scene – it doesn't matter.

From the
famous nude
scene in *Darling*

And she said, "But it does matter. I will be unattractive and people will see me." You see, *she does* want everybody to adore her!'

In Christie's own account, to Tony Crawley, she admits that she planned never to do the scene. 'I read the script and thought, well, I won't do *that.* Impossible! Then nearer the time, I brought it up. I said, John, you don't mean to . . . er? And he said, Oh yes, I do. And I said, Oh no, I just couldn't. Oh no, please. And it went on like that. Right up to the day we shot it. I would have walked off the film if I could have done . . . It was ghastly.'

When the day came Christie wept, but she did the scene. The set was cleared, she stripped naked and Schlesinger had what he wanted in one take. A few minutes, no more. 'She was,' he says, 'one hundred percent professional.' To shore up her ego, he invited her to the day's rushes. She watched herself shyly, blushing, and admitted, *sotto voce,* that she 'wasn't bad'. Discussion and argument ended, and the film coursed ahead, hindered now only by continuing persistent cash flow problems.

Darling was nearing completion – and bankruptcy – when a miracle occurred. Janni and Anglo-Amalgamated's Nat Cohen had begun to doubt their chances of finishing the picture when, out of the blue, David Lean called Christie's agents. Lean was interested in Christie and impressed that other producers had been able, however shakily, to build a major production around her. He was anxious, he said, to see some footage of *Darling.* It was common knowledge that Lean was casting an epic version of Pasternak's *Dr Zhivago* and involvement with the film, bush telegraph decreed, was tantamount to winning the pools. It would be, rumour had it, the most lavish, expensive production of the decade. A surefire hit before a foot of film was in the can. The booming reputations of Lean, Pasternak, screenwriter Robert Bolt and cinematographer Freddie Young clinched the case.

Every agent everywhere, Hollywood and London, was scrambling with offers and suggestions. But Lean wanted to see Christie and, perhaps a little less enthusiastically, Bogarde. Bogarde's friend, the director Joseph Losey, sent some footage of *King and Country* and Janni, recognizing the smell of salvation, sent the best bits of *Darling.* Everyone waited with bated breath for Lean's reaction – that is, everyone except Julie Christie. She didn't seem more than mildly concerned and, although aware that *Darling* could collapse in financial disarray, adamantly refused to wallow in the excitement of Lean's interest and the implications in terms of Janni's fifty percent cut of any offered salary. Bessant and her mates in Kensington were, if anything, keener.

A few agonizing weeks passed, then the expected phone call came. *Darling* was still shooting – this time at location on the lawns of Skindles in Maidenhead. Christie was clad in tweed suit and pearls,

Darling

radiant for her role, but reading Karl Marx during breaks. The phone call came, she drifted off then returned to her fellow actors with the news. Bogarde was still awaiting his summons – a call which never did come. He watched a serene Christie approach across the trim lawn.

'Well, what happened?'

She only shrugged. 'I've got Lara. Rather good.'

But she didn't seem pleased. She sat down and thumbed out her page in Karl Marx while Bogarde watched on, slack-jawed, waiting for the bad news. 'Problem is,' Christie resumed, 'they want me to get out of this *little* picture . . . said that it wasn't important and that I should go to Madrid, where they're based, as soon as possible, to start working on the part.' The temporary serenity was replaced by a grim-set expression and, as Bogarde recalls, she slammed her book and flung it into the grass in annoyance. 'They say I could get an Oscar for Lara, that I should leave John and this one.'

'And so?' Bogarde asked.

'And so what!' She was, says Bogarde, almost crying with the affront. 'I told them to stuff Lara or wait. They'll bloody have to wait. Leave this? Leave John, all this! What kind of business do they think this is?'

Lean had got off to a bad start. Six months before, in the vacuum of renewed rep, still nursing the wounds of Independent Artists, Christie might easily have junked *Zhivago* aside. But whether she liked the proferred new set-up or not, she knew she had to play along if she was to serve Schlesinger and Janni's interests. Janni had meetings with her and urged her to quick acceptance. He explained the benefits of association with Lean in terms of a firmer market footing for her: side by side *Darling* and *Zhivago*, gems from different ends of the movie spectrum, would fuse into one glorious fortune of publicity. And this time it would be the right sort of publicity, tempered by the unquestionable integrity of the respective productions. More urgently, Janni stressed, he needed the cash. Christie understood and agreed. Months later Janni unashamedly confessed: 'I sold Julie Christie to David Lean. The deal paid her salary (for *Darling*), she got a share of the profits and the rest of the money completed *Darling*.'

Several interiors and 'pick-up shots' had yet to be filmed for *Darling* but, eager to assist Lean (and Christie), Janni allowed her to fly to Madrid before Christmas. She left in a mood of some optimism, not cocky about her work on *Darling* but coolly confident: a confidence arising more from the fact that she had survived the production than anything else.

Schlesinger kissed her goodbye and wished her luck. He was happy with the results of her labours and more than a little sad to see her go.

For a start, he didn't envy her the gruelling one-year production schedule lined up for *Zhivago*. No doubt he wondered would she cope.

His concern was fond rather than professional. In rebuilding Julie Christie – making her a true-grit star – he had also made a dear friend. Many times during the film he'd had occasion to doubt her affection and appreciation of what he had set out to achieve. But her Christmas present to him banished all doubts. The label on the simple gift read:

To my dear John from his Trilby, with love.

She forgave him for the nudity and the tears. She understood.

1965, the year of searing success, began with good cheer. Julie Christie felt she was learning her way, proving herself, growing up. Within the business she had won good admirers.

It is easy to miss the genius behind Schlesinger's, Janni's and Raphael's concept for *Darling*. Though some notable critics latterly panned it – for the Elkan Allans in 1980 it was 'overrated . . . Schlesinger's skill only partly conceals emptiness of the film' – most have consistently if insufficiently sung its praise. *Darling* was released in the late summer of '65, appropriately the highpoint and fulcrum of the Swinging Sixties. Its aim, in an unadorned and cynical fashion, was to lay bare the heart of Sixties' values through the focus of one complex character, Diana, the working-class kid made good. The Sixties marked the end of thirteen years of Tory government and the emergence of a Labour administration which, in its pledge for dynamic action, triggered a social revolt. Youth culture was born, centred on pop music, fashion and sexual freedom – but founded on the soft sand of whimsicality.

For the first time, it became fashionable to be working-class and the cinema pandered to the moment, churning out rough-hewn backstreet heroes like Michael Caine and Terence Stamp. The *Darling* persona captured the essence of this butterfly culture and exposed its pretence and graver weaknesses. As the writer Jeffrey Richards observed, *Darling* was destined to become the Sixties in aspic, a slashing denunciation of a media-dominated environment 'hungry for new sensations, in which style was more important than content and individual self-expression took precedence over the corporate values of family, political party, class, religion or nation.' Everything about the movie echoed the texture of the time: the glittering black and white photography, the tone of pseudo moralistic self-analysis, the ambiguity struck by a blend of parody, irony and satire, the confusion, the hope. In every sense the film was a doom-laden microcosm of Swinging England and, as such, unveiled and merciless, it could easily have been vilified – or simply ignored.

A year earlier its unhappy fate might well have been sealed but '65 was a turn-around year, a dizzy reckless pinnacle from which there could only be decline. And so *Darling* was absorbed and adored. Those still soaked in the hedonism of the era thrived on the

Sunday-supplement content – glamour, drugs and orgies in Paris; the more discerning swooned to the ironies. Both groups adopted the sexy, mini-skirted Diana as their standard-bearer and elevated Julie Christie to a place with the fashionable gods – the Beatles, David Bailey, Vidal Sassoon. She was the first female all-British all-purpose sixties icon, symbol of rebellion and success, rebellion and decline.

The movie-world, from whichever motive or understanding, promptly honoured Schlesinger and Christie. Within weeks of its American release *Darling* was earmarked for Oscars and Julie Christie had 'arrived' on the international scene. British reaction was good, but the American critics positively erupted in ecstasy with hardly one dissenting voice. Most of the praise was lavished on Christie. *Life* magazine, which would soon give cover space to the 'new British import', applauded 'a performance of pure gold. By turns wilful and willing, intelligent and self-deceiving, innocent and teasing – it is a characterization such as one rarely sees.' The *New York World Telegram* baldly stated, 'Julie Christie is brilliant . . . the character feels or fakes every emotion known to woman. Miss Christie manages

Bathing beauties in *Darling*

them all.' And the esteemed *Herald-Tribune* foresaw the start of something wonderful: 'The girl is a delight with her mobile child-and-sorceress face . . . *Darling* will put Julie Christie up there among the celluloid goddesses.'

The flood was endless and justified Janni's calculation that America was the country to premiere in, that its distance from the British scene would provide a valuable objectivity. In Britain, on release at the beginning of September, just as expected some daggers were drawn. *The Times* saw Schlesinger's point but arrogantly ignored the ironies. Comparison with Fellini's *La Dolce Vita* was made with the conclusion that 'the strength of Fellini's film, unmatched here, was that it constantly assumed there was a preferable alternative to the life it condemned'. At the same time Schlesinger's gift for exposé was approved. But in fact, in Schlesinger's eyes, there seemed no ready remedy for Diana's troubles; derision for traditional conformity was as much implicit as anything. *Darling* used parody and satire to propose a question; it assumed nothing, certainly presumed no answers. *The Guardian,* ridiculously, believed Schlesinger had 'chosen too big a canvas'. Ian Wright rambled on: 'There is a destructiveness about Schlesinger's moral indictment of affluence . . . Character, particularly the girl's, is distorted to the point at which one wants to cry out: People don't behave like that.' Christie, though, he quite liked, but the patronizing tone harked back to best-forgotten days: 'Always attractive to watch, [she] is set a perverse standard of bitterness which cuts across a naturally attractive effervescence.'

Christie, by now in lonely exile in Spain, many months into the impossibly strained *Dr Zhivago,* missing Bessant and England and her midnight mates, was upset when the home reviews came. 'I was hurt,' she admitted later. 'I felt let down by my own country . . . it's not good to feel one's own country thinks little of one.' By contrast, American reaction inspired her to untypical vocal excitement. For the first time she matched the critics pace for pace in enthusiasm. She sought and received regular reports on *Darling*'s progress around the world and was patently gratified by a good box-office and the splendid American personal notices.

She told Tony Crawley: 'The reviews in England were all wrong, in the United States they were more perceptive. For instance, the English critics kept complaining about how *nice* Diana was . . . too nice to behave the way she did, and so on. But she wouldn't have got anywhere if she hadn't known how to be an absolute darling. That was the point!' If anything, Christie's willingness to promote *Darling,* however restricted by the heavy pressures of Lean's film, *grew* in inverse proportion to the British *anti* press. Maybe, at last, she believed she had achieved a screen success compatible with her ambitions – which seems likely.

But there were other factors. The signs were that she had cracked the essential American market. Though still only twenty-four independence and ultimate autonomy were her urgent goals. Janni had contractual power over her for another three years and might wish to extend that, but it was increasingly clear that whatever success she made under his fosterage could be laid as the foundation for a strongly self-styled future career. Money, of course, would help and the palpable evidence of the value of the Janni-Schlesinger ticket was there already: her fee for *Darling* was $7,500. Months later, for *Zhivago*, it was a staggering $120,000. And Janni was already scouting out new projects for her, toying with his own ideas as well as stirring the interest of other producers with fat chequebooks.

Talking to flocks of visiting reporters from her star dressing-room in the new CEA Studios near Madrid, Christie loyally placed herself in the Janni-Schlesinger camp and acknowledged her debt of gratitude and their tutelage. She was suddenly prepared to be proud of her work – not just for herself but for her mentors too. At the same time a sudden impenetrable curtain came down on her private life. She told successive visiting journalists: 'I will not talk about Don Bessant . . . marriage doesn't interest me . . . I've nothing more to say.' It seemed that the isolation of long weeks in Spain had afforded her time to mull upon and finally cast a new crusty mould which would be a shield from henceforth, protecting her fragile secret self. Donald Zec, frequent easy friend to the stars, found her a tricky interview, 'as much your conventional movie star as, say Zsa Zsa Gabor is like Edward Heath.' After a string of aborted questions he found himself deducing, 'Call her star and she winces. Call her an actress and she will gladly buy you the next round of stouts. But do not call her 'darling'. Miss Christie is really not that type of girl.'

Apart from keen concern for *Darling* and initial difficulties settling into Lean's style of working, Christie had reason to be happy. In her private life events were trundling happily. Bessant, in her absence, had found a well-paid teaching post at the Maidstone School of Art in Kent and kept in touch daily by phone. Brother Clive and mother Rosemary occupied the London flat when the mates weren't around and put the place in some order. In the summer everyone took the opportunity to holiday in Spain and keep Julie company. She wept tears at Bessant's arrival, claiming she had been desperately lonely too long. Some friends followed out and a festive party mood entered *Zhivago* for the first time.

'In the beginning,' she said, 'I hated it here. I was lonely and bored . . . but things changed when my friends came out. It was good.' Shortly after Bessant's holiday an engagement was announced, giving cause for Roderick Mann to congratulate her weeks later in London, over tea at Fortnum's. She didn't deny the engagement but 'looked

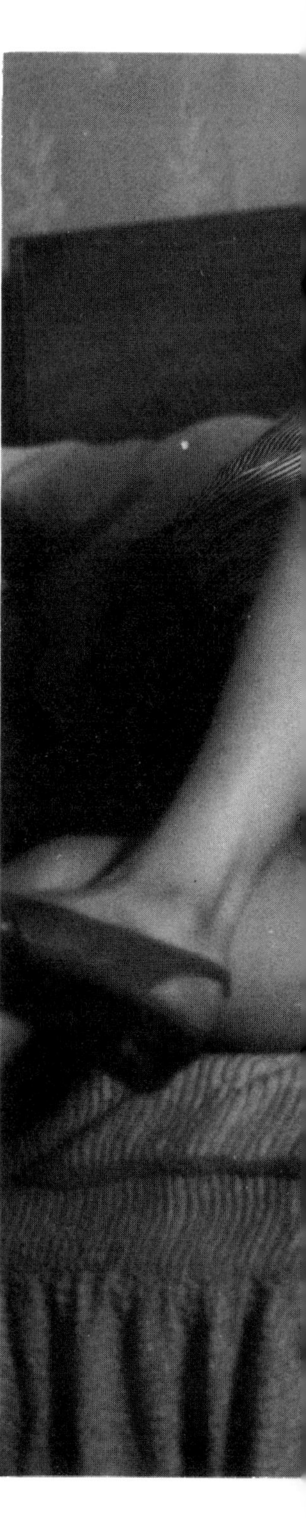

Previous page: Christie and Bogarde in *Darling*

flustered'. She broke her own vow of silence to tell Mann: 'To be honest with you, I don't see myself getting married. I'm always serious when I start a new friendship, but not for long. I know it won't last. Honestly, I don't think I could give myself utterly to one man . . . There are so many temptations [in showbusiness], even if you are a good person. And I am not a good person.'

Bessant probably laughed that off as sweetly as Christie did. Their love was surer than ever and, under the pressure of *Darling*'s success and Lean's tough direction, she needed him more than ever. A few sporty writers did try to corner Bessant and plumb the relationship a little further, but they failed to elicit anything worth a one-inch column in the cheapest paper. The more discerning accepted the fact: Christie had taken her cue from this new stardom to draw a full and final veil over gossipy self-revealing interviews. All she would ever freely discuss from now on – and irregularly and inarticulately at that – was her work. Greater areas of vulnerability would be concealed forever. Schlesinger deserved analysis and thanks and she was happy to play along. But she was keen to speculate on Fellini, Godard and Renoir too – not shy to openly wonder at her chances of netting a part in the next movie by Fellini, or maybe Sidney Lumet ('the only American I admire'). She was, unusually, presumptuous. The scales of judgement on *Darling* had yet to settle. The Oscar nominations drew near but Stanley Kauffman was cautious in *The New Republic:* 'She has an expressive, unusual face and a not unattractive voice, but she is not yet a controlled or subtle actress. Her chief effects come from her vivid personality in this tailor-made part.'

Christie read this, worst of the few sour American notices, and was alerted. Heart, soul and sinew went into the last months of *Zhivago*. 'I never used to want to be a star,' she told Roderick Mann with surprising vehemence. 'But now I do. I realize I've got something that maybe could be made good. You can't just laugh off a thing like that. So now I don't say anymore I don't want to be a star. It just wouldn't be true. *I do.*'

She would outgrow Janni-Schlesinger soon enough, everyone knew, but the confusion remained: where exactly were her sights fixed now? What would she be without them?

OF DINOSAURS AND DARLING DREAMS

The mounting of *Dr Zhivago,* the greatest of the dinosaur supermovies of the sixties, was a logistical nightmare that involved 800 craftsmen working for more than two years in three countries, at a final production cost of more than $14 million – twice the budget allotted by the backers, MGM. But *Zhivago* heralded a new breed of supermovie – up-to-date historical drama phrased in Victorian romanticism, miles away from the simple spectacle of *Cleopatra* (1963). It proved its worth by taking nearly $20 million in its first six months. Ultimately, along with the takings of the dusted-down and reissued *Gone With the Wind* (1939), *Zhivago* was responsible for keeping MGM alive and viable at a time when, in the midst of management wrangles and colossal flops, the company looked like going under.

From the start, ironically, it seemed an unlikely subject and MGM had reservations. Boris Pasternak's novel was the very stuff of bad movies: convoluted, episodic, poetic. But Pasternak had been awarded the Nobel prize on the strength of the book and the controversy sparked by the Soviet authorities' refusal to allow the author to accept his prize brought a notoreity that gripped the public imagination.* Carlo Ponti had meanwhile made an agreeable arrangement with Pasternak's Italian publishers and David Lean, fresh from the enormous hit *Lawrence of Arabia* (1962) expressed immediate interest. So the package was prepared and locations sought.

---

*Pasternak's book was published first in Italy, after the Soviets had decided it was anti-Communist, in 1957. On October 23, 1958 the official announcement of the Nobel prize was made but Pasternak, a lover of Russia, was told he could never return to Moscow if he flew to Sweden to accept the prize. He died, embittered, in 1960, at Peredelkino, near Moscow.

Doctor Zhivago

At first the production was planned for Hollywood, but costs were crippling. Spain had recently emerged as an economical alternative – where weather was good and labour twice as plentiful – so the film was re-sited to CEA Studios and a ten-acre plain which would be developed as a backlot near Madrid airport. The story was set round the time of the Russian revolution and period authenticity, Lean decided, must be paramount. To that end, production designer John Box (also responsible for the lushness of *Lawrence of Arabia*), took his 800-man crew through a hectic eighteen months of reconstructing Moscow outside Madrid. The giant exterior set comprised a half-mile long, paved street, complete with operational tram lines and dominated by an accurate replica of the Kremlin. There was also a functional viaduct, with railway engines, a church, and more than fifty business premises.

Other gigantic sets were built in the mountains near Sona, north of Madrid, an area topographically similar to the Steppes of Russia. Here it was necessary to alter the course of a river, no less, to fit requirements and miles of fresh railway tracks were laid. Further construction work took place in Finland and among Canada's Rocky Mountains. In all, Lean and Box employed 120 plasterers, 210 carpenters, sixty masons, twenty-five tubular steel specialists, thirty painters, twenty electricians and more than 300 back-up technicians – just to prepare the way for shooting.

Phase two involved top-grade casting, and Lean was fortunate in that his pre-eminent position among Hollywood directors allowed him to choose not just instantly bankable stars. His 'old reliables', Alec Guinness, Ralph Richardson and Omar Sharif, were courted once more, but the casting of Geraldine Chaplin and Julie Christie caused some concern. MGM were reportedly less than happy about Christie, though it must be remembered that Lean was casting her on the strength of film scraps – the glimpses of *Darling* and short performances like *Young Cassidy* that gave no evidence of her capacity for featured playing. But he told MGM and the rest of the world: 'I picked her because of the five (sic) minute scene she had in *Billy Liar*. In that small amount of footage she gave every evidence of being an outstanding actress.' MGM, it's fair to guess, were still edgy when, very early in the day, Robert H. O'Brien, president of the company, was gamely announcing: 'We at Metro-Goldwyn Mayer are proud of our tradition of bringing the finest in screen entertainment to motion picture audiences around the world. *Doctor Zhivago* is a notable addition to this distinguished roster.'

Christie's awareness of MGM's doubts, combined with Lean's forbidding reputation as a hard-driving director, made the first part of *Zhivago* an agonizing experience. Rod Steiger, who would share lead billing, arrived in Spain to find 'a frightened little bird' grappling with

the slow spiralling build-up of *Darling* and expectations for *Zhivago*. He didn't fully understand her and grew no closer than other co-stars before him but, like Bogarde and Harvey, he learned to admire her, relaying word to *Newsweek* of her 'immense courage to face all this.'

David Lean, on the other hand, first discovered a tetchy, too-modern miss and must have wondered if he had indeed miscast this key role of Lara. She was, by all reports, sometimes giddy, often too self-assertive, and alternately loud-mouthed and coy about her success in *Darling*. It took several weeks before any note of amicable partnership was struck.

Christie later remarked: 'David is tremendously disciplined. He couldn't stand me fooling around. I don't change my ways for anyone, but as the part became more difficult I submitted myself to him completely. I learned discipline.'

As the production moved to Joensuu, Eastern Finland, just seventy-five miles from the Russian border, to shoot snowbound exteriors in temperatures of 30° below, Lean was still unsure about his star female choice. The kindest thing he could say about her was that she was 'an independent creature with strong views of her own' – but he made no concessions to her; rather, like Schlesinger, kept up a badgering relentless pressure.

After shooting on frozen Lake Phyaselka, it was back to Spain and summer temperatures that hovered around 120°. Momentarily Christie broke down. She'd had little or no time to herself since the beginning of *Darling* and was emotionally at her dangerous weakest. For a while, just as on *Darling*, arguments flared and tears were shed. Lean shouted at her and she collapsed in tears. 'I'm terribly serious about my work,' she said. 'Though I'm sure David doesn't realize it. He thinks I'm a bit of a scatterbrain. He'd prefer me to act more like a star, but I can't. . .'

Relations with Omar Sharif, fledgling matinee idol supreme, were reportedly unstable. On screen, as Yuri Zhivago and dressmaker's daughter Lara, the couple brewed up a tempestuous, enthralling romance. But in real life the chemistry was somewhat different. Cairo-born Sharif complained: 'She'd eat fried egg sandwiches for elevenses, which for me is totally unromantic. Nothing wrong with friend egg sandwiches – except that they're rather unfeminine.' Christie, however, kept a tight rein on the working relationship, instinctively knowing the risks of open war on a second front. Seventeen years later, queried about Sharif by the *Daily Mirror*, she was decently vague. Not only could she not recall the sandwiches, but she had difficulty remembering Sharif. 'He was charming, but otherwise I don't remember anything about him really . . . I can't even remember if I have ever met him since.'

Lean's demands for her to 'act like a star' were misinterpreted. In

Previous page: In *Doctor Zhivago* with Tom Courtney, whom Christie first worked with on *Billy Liar*

truth, all he wanted was glitzy star acting – the emotional high fizz to match a peppy epic. The problem was, for many months the demands exceeded her perception and versatility. She simply had not the experience, so she was forced to pipe down, forget the discomforts of heat and loneliness, and listen and learn. By the time *Darling* went on release her months of dutiful study had come good and she was performing better than ever, demonstrating a good sense of 'epic' acting.

The summer holiday visits of Bessant and her friends had helped assuage her discontent and a solid friendship with Lean, based on mutual understanding, developed. He visited her at her cramped one-bedroom apartment near the Madrid studios and was quick with encouragement when she made script suggestions. He even obtained a pre-premiere print of *Darling* for which he arranged a special screening, with Julie as guest of honour. She sat shy and timid through the screening, biting her nails, cringing and bursting into laughter by turns – and in the end found herself pleased with the applause, happy with herself. Her affections swung. She hugged Lean. She basked in his honest attentiveness and went from strength to strength.

'This was a process that would be often repeated through the years,' says an associate. 'The director as father-figure. Maybe it had something to do with the fact that her parents split when she was still a child, that her recollections of her father were remote, never much talked about. I think Schlesinger became a father-figure, and the same happened with Lean. She resisted in the beginning because that was her way – she was a tough child, a child *made* tough by an unconventional upbringing. But she hungered for a father, a strong man, someone to look up to, to *yield* to.'

Bessant, many noted, hardly fitted the tough man image. By Christie's own definition he was 'quiet', while she was extrovert and hard-talking. But, on *Zhivago,* she had told visiting American writer Helen Lawrenson, 'The most important thing in a man-woman relationship is for the man to be the dominant one. This is what Don and I have . . . his values are my values.' She made a point of stressing that Bessant was, artistically at least, as strong as her: not only was he teaching in Kent now, he had also got part-time employment at St Martin's Art School in London, a worthy post. 'He isn't just an art teacher,' Christie insisted, 'he's a painter – and a good painter.' His pictures, she said, were hung in her flat, his future was great.

But her defence of him was vigorous and, some observed, cast a truer light on the relationship. She was, she told Lawrenson, outraged that journalists in Britain had been hounding Bessant for a story, following the on-off engagement announcement. Glib statements he had made contradicted her remarks to people like Roderick Mann. Far as he was concerned, apparently, marriage was in the offing.

'Those bastards!' Christie told Lawrenson, referring to the London Press corps. 'I told them not to call up Don. They promised they wouldn't . . . I can't stand them asking him questions about us. He loathes that sort of thing . . . We've talked about marriage, of course, and we've talked about having children . . . But marriage seems like signing yourself away for life. I just don't *know*.'

She was more at ease, as always now, speculating on her career. She told Lawrenson she was still interested in theatre, and would love to play Hilda in *The Master Builder*. But affection for theatre was not the main motivation. Its restrictive conditions would help her 'not lose my perspective at all those dreadful, corrupting astronomical sums of money film people flash at you'. The corollary for her was straightforward: 'Then perhaps I can sort out my private life.'

But the drawbacks of fame and exposure with the twin explosions of *Darling* and *Zhivago* were correspondingly greater than anything she'd suffered from the milder successes of the Annakin days. Accountants, agents, sub-agents, and PR people of every description and variety popped out of the woodwork like so many mice. No sooner was *Zhivago* completed in early autumn than an expansive schedule of promotion work and further film assignments was thrown before her. Schlesinger announced she would have a small part in his planned film, *A Severed Head*, to be followed by a Thomas Hardy epic, *Far From the Madding Crowd*, billed from the start as 'the most expensive British production of the coming year'.

She was also persuaded to appear in a TV commercial for hair conditioner but conceded, she said, only because her fee was exactly the same as her bank overdraft. After *Zhivago* and estimated in-pocket earnings of about £40,000 (after Janni's cut) it seemed inconceivable that she had debts – but she claimed she did. The support of her swelling band of freewheeling mates drained her purse, she said. She wasn't bitter about this; if anything, she was proud. 'People help you when you're down – you should help them when you can.' It is possible that her acceptance of yet another hurried major film part grew from such financial exigencies, though the facts weigh more in favour of this burgeoning desire to gain respectable, manageable celebrity.

In late autumn she agreed to star in Francois Truffaut's *Fahrenheit 451*, a science-fiction feature, slotted to start shooting in Pinewood on January 10th. Before that there was a U.S. promotion tour to correspond with the Christmas opening of *Zhivago* in New York, and protracted discussions with her agent, Olive Harding of London Artists, who was negotiating a clever deal with solicitor Stanley Gorrie 'to minimise the tax problems' of what was promising to be a long and rich career. Ultimately the deal fixed between Christie's agents and lawyers proved more trouble than it was worth, forming the basis of

what was called 'the most controversial tax avoidance case ever to hit the High Court' – a case so intricate that even the esteemed *Daily Telegraph* finance writers covering the Court of Appeal hearing in 1976 got lost in the details and classed it 'one of the most complex and elaborate tax avoidance schemes ever witnessed'. Christie herself, it seems, was baffled by the scheme too – but she signed because she was told it made sense, would multiply her earnings and gain her freedom beyond Janni.

Essentially she entered into an agreement with a quickly shuffled-up company called Rosebroom in which she undertook to serve them exclusively as an actress for seven years at a salary of £7,500 rising to £13,500. (Inherent in the arrangement presumably was a let-out which allowed her to continue with Janni till his contract lapsed.) The remaining fat earnings, which would normally command a high rate of direct tax, she was divested of, and they were exchanged for receipts (created out of those earnings) which in turn were transmuted into capital receipts. These latter were not subject to tax. The formula was known as 'the open commercial trust scheme', devised by a well-known solicitor. Its application in Christie's case, however, eventually led to litigation and controversy – though Christie emerged unscathed in the end.

Amidst such tangled, half-fixed plans, Christie flew off to the States for her second visit – this time in more auspicious circumstances. MGM feted her and the showbiz chroniclers rained down, heated with the hint of an approaching Oscar for *Darling*. *Time* called her 'irresistible', *The New Yorker* burbled ecstatically about 'the ravishing Julie Christie, the beautiful Julie Christie', *Newsweek* believed she epitomized the spirit of freedom – 'freedom from care, convention, celebration, civilization, freedom from others and even from one's self'.

Christie, meanwhile, was on the verge of collapse. She dutifully met the top brass interviewers and spoke rapturously about Lean and the upcoming *Zhivago*. She pushed *Darling* and always remembered to mention Schlesinger. And all the time Bessant sat by her side, buoying her at the worst moments but withdrawing appropriately when the limelight blazed and those precious moments of new-sanctified 'freedom' were frozen in photo print. *Newsweek* ranted breathlessly:

> On the phone she paces like a lioness, tossing her mane from side to side. In a nightgown, she looks like a pathetic orphan; togged in a Mary Quant outfit she is an impish schoolgirl. Her voice, normally a sexy purr, can escalate to tantrum sharpness, and her boarding-school English is well seasoned with Anglo-Saxonisms.

Under the ad-man's gloss lurked a large uncomfortable truth. The

Previous page: As Lara in *Doctor Zhivago* with Omar Sharif as Yuri tantrums were real and regular, symptomatic of the exhaustion. The foul language was the readiest safety vent. Early in December when *Newsweek*'s Irwin Goodwin visited her in West Kensington he found 'photographers holding her at bay . . . and Julie was frantic'. At one juncture, checking her appointments' diary to make yet another photo call arrangement she broke down and cried: 'Oh God, I have no time for myself!'

Dr Zhivago premiered on December 22 in New York but its reception took Christie by surprise. MGM liked it enough and the paying public were pleased, but the critics were less than eager to take the ritual baton of hype. Four months later, starting with a charity premiere attended by Princess Margaret and Lord Snowdon, the film opened its British run to similar mixed response. For the *Monthly Film Bulletin* it was, quite simply, 'an honest failure' and Christie could do no better than 'struggle conscientiously' with the part of Lara. In retrospect, probably too much was expected of *Zhivago*. The screenwriter Robert Bolt himself pointed out that only about one twenty-fourth of Pasternak's novel was used for the film – and yet his screenplay published by Random House in the States ran to a massive 224 pages. Significantly too, many expected *Zhivago* to carry a political message and reckoned Lean and Bolt evaded important socio-political issues. Bolt loudly contested this assertion, claiming that Pasternak's novel was apolitical, a story of love and honour, no more.

As Lean filmed it, *Dr Zhivago* follows the life of a young poet-doctor, the character of the title (Sharif) who marries impulsively then, after a succession of casual meetings over many years – years of the Great War and Russian revolution – falls in love with the proud and hard-headed Larissa Fyodorovna. Zhivago and Lara's love and commitment to each other is at last expressed, but political upheaval separates them and in the end Zhivago dies, still searching for his lover, on the streets of war-torn Moscow. Lara disappears into a labour camp but gives birth to their child (Rita Tushingham) who lives to tell the tale to Yevgraf (Alec Guinness).

In their reviews *The Times* and *Variety* respectively found the film too slow to start and too drawn-out in its finale, though both admired Christie. *The Times* felt she reaffirmed her screen presence and *Variety* restored the superlatives of *Darling*: '[She] is outstanding in a sensitive, yet earthy and full-blooded portrayal.' But that was the best of the crop. Other reviewers thought the film weak and Christie ineffective. In fact, its weaknesses probably grew from the political climate of the middle sixties – the post-Cuba, thawing-Cold-War climate that begged for a sympathetic reappraisal of Soviet Russia. Lean complied, but with subtlety, distilling the human values of love and passion to the point where they achieve such potency that awkward political and social issues are neutralized totally. Hence, for some, the appearance of an uncaring film – inappropriate when ranged beside the degradation suffered by its true author, Pasternak.

Winging back to London for New Year '66 and the excitements already lined up – Truffaut, and *Far from the Madding Crowd* – Christie displayed an ominous reflex reaction to the glitter of America which had, in so many ways, seemed an extension of the Annakin-Beaconsfield days. *Zhivago* she suddenly categorized as some sort of personal failure. She told one reporter: 'I didn't enjoy making the film . . . but the people in it were very pleasant. Geraldine Chaplin in particular has that rare quality of being liked by women as much as men . . . but somehow I felt very out of it. I was very alone.' She told *Woman*: 'Playing Lara presented a terrific problem. She was a woman with a terrific maturity and it was difficult for me to play her because I'm not particularly mature, and I'm quite a jerky person . . . I don't think I've made her alive and light enough.'

The discontentment which was really disappointment at *Zhivago* – which once more essentially underlined her unpreparedness for big-time exposure – was stifling now. She became ill over New Year and dramatically lost weight. A doctor was consulted and she was ordered to rest, but she found it hard to unwind. The flat provided some distraction – now there was a cat called Doggy, eight finches and two potted palms to tend to – but scripts piled up on the living-room table, summoning. Close friends feared a full-blown nervous breakdown but Christie wisely escaped to Wales, away from the furore. Rosemary and Clive had moved to Wales, to a two-storey white-stone cottage in Llanafan, near Aberystwyth, surrounded by high birches and bleak hills. It was the ideal sanatorium at this time, and would be the sanctum of escape in many future crises.

Undeterred by the lukewarm initial response to *Zhivago*, MGM forged ahead with a devilishly smart, unremitting promotion campaign. Comparison with *War and Peace* and *Gone with the Wind* became key-phrase copy in all handouts and Christie's face, regal and serene as Lara, was the emblem of the noble movie. Cinema managers everywhere were supplied with booklets outlining the historic importance of the film that pompously instructed:

> 'The National Anthem should be played *before* the screening of *Dr Zhivago* as this will avoid the undignified scramble which often results in marring the end of a public performance. No other music should be played at any time during your engagement of the film except that which comes off the soundtrack. To do so would completely destroy the mood . . . There are to be no concession sales (chocolate, cigarettes, ices, etc) during the performance of *Dr Zhivago* . . . Make certain that all your staff are fully aware of their duties and that if they remain in the auditorium during the

screening, they do not talk, flash their torches or move about unnecessarily – a whispering or wandering usherette can be most disconcerting to patrons.'

All of which, in light of the critics' reaction, seemed fatuous and a time-waste. Some predicted *Zhivago* would flop hugely within months. But MGM's confidence paid off: in the 1966 Academy Awards, the film took Oscars for Best Screenplay from Another Medium, Cinematography, Art Direction, Set Direction, Costume Design and Music. In a matter of a short few years its earnings crossed the $100 million mark and today it hovers around tenth position on the chart of all-time box-office hits.

Christie, meanwhile, was struggling with her health and temporarily uninterested in the movie world. Some associates claim she contemplated quitting movies completely, but she was already contracted to Universal and Truffaut for *Fahrenheit 451,* to begin within days. The fact that Universal, who had refused to purchase her for *The War Lord* at $35,000 just two years earlier, were now happily forking out something reportedly close to $200,000 did not excite her. Even Janni's gentle goading found little response. But the commitment to Truffaut pushed her towards recuperation and optimism. She was, she told friends, very flattered that he had chosen her. The breadth of her appeal to good movie directors was frightening and reassuring all at once. And, after the pressure and relative failure (in her eyes) of *Zhivago,* she badly needed reassurance. At heart, no one disputed, she still wanted to act, and win praise.

But the year's exile in Spain and the American promotion tour brought about important changes. From the security of Bessant's arms she told the world: 'I'm not a gypsy now. I like my home.' In that wavering moment, quite possibly, she came nearer to marriage than she ever would with Bessant. But the moment passed, and she rediscovered her health and confidence.

Truffaut was frustrated in his attempts to start *Fahrenheit* on January 10th because of Christie's slow recovery. An insurance company's doctor, engaged by Universal, checked her over and found her unready for work. She was, the doctor concluded, suffering severe exhaustion and needed a wisdom tooth pulled. It was hoped she might be fit to start in a week, but the shadow of her illness was serious enough to cost Truffaut more than one night's sleep. In his personal journal of the film, reprinted in *Cahiers du Cinema,* Truffaut expressed quiet fears that Universal might cancel the $1 million movie. He was consoled only by the fact that hundreds of thousands of dollars worth of futuristic sets had been built at Pinewood, and the company was unlikely to call it a day after such expenditure without at least giving its leading lady a second try.

Finally, on Monday January 17th, Truffaut started rolling on his first

British movie. Christie was still confined to bed, sleeping round the clock, taking care of her diet, striving to build back the lost weight. On January 31st, much later than anyone expected, she was ready to work: 'terrified, almost paralysed,' in her account. The slow process of 'discovering' her director – as happened with Schlesinger and Lean – started all over again. It was made easier this time by her ability to converse in French with Truffaut, whose English was poor. She felt herself to be starting with an advantage and her courage rose. In his journal Truffaut starkly noted: 'Julie was jittery but she came through well.'

In February when the nominations for the Oscars were announced, Julie Christie and *Darling* were duly there. In March the British Film Academy named her Best Actress for *Darling*. To this was added New York Critics' Best Actress award. On April 16th she was due in Hollywood for the Oscars ceremony. Throughout the spring her health had steadily improved and Truffaut was much pleased with her. Her idiosyncratic ways and oddball friends amused him. 'Everyone on the unit likes Julie,' he wrote, 'as opposed to her co-partner [Oskar Werner]. She has many friends who often come to watch her shooting, and every time she first asked my permission. The last time, I told her that it was marvellous to have so many friends, and I added: It's a funny thing – one never sees any of Oskar's friends on the set. She replied with a sweet smile: "That's because we're not shooting in Austria" [Werner's homeland].' Truffaut had had trouble striking a rapport with Werner and Christie's gentle humour in the circumstances suggested a new awareness, a focus away from herself.

On her birthday, April 14th, her last day of shooting was marked with a boozy celebration arranged by Truffaut. A day later, she was on her way to Hollywood and the Oscars. Unready, as ever.

With director François Truffaut on the set of *Fahrenheit 451*

TO

THE OSCAR IDYLL

'When they told me I might have to go to Hollywood because they might give me an Oscar I . . . I was overcome, terrified. I was persuaded to go at last. I got on the plane and, suddenly, found myself in that enormous theatre, with all those famous people, stars, the President's daughter. I felt out of place, ridiculous, among all those people so different from me. Then I heard my name called. That was worse than anything. I kept wondering, Why me? I stood up and I didn't know where to go or what to do. I only felt a great wish to laugh. No, to cry . . . no, both.'

Jet-lagged and clinging to Bessant, Christie had braved the tensions of Hollywood's greatest honours ceremony admirably. She was hot favourite for the Best Actress award and entered the Los Angeles Music Centre knock-kneed with the fear of what seemed inevitable – the winning. Three thousand showbiz denizens crowded the vast tiered hall and TV cameras swung round, televising to the nation. Rex Harrison ambled on stage to announce the Best Actress and Christie's nails bit deep into Bessant's hand. She was, appropriately, dressed in gold from head to toe – an immaculate silky evening gown made specially in London. She hated the occasion and loved it. She sweated and trembled. She wanted to win, and didn't. Harrison tore open the envelope and she was momentarily distracted by the flurry of activity as rostrum cameras swivelled to search out important faces, looking for expression and contrast. Harrison was talking and she didn't hear him. 'I just sat there and saw the TV cameras moving about and I thought, Oh well, that's it. It's not me. Maybe some other time. . .'

Despite herself, despite her reluctance to be here, the feeling of naked exposure, the terrible razzle-dazzle, she wanted Julie Christie to be honoured. She needed to be told she was making her way, making progress, getting good. 'I was hoping for me,' she told English journalist Ann Buchanan hazily. 'I wanted to win. I want to be different, and I guess I am – a little.'

With the Oscar she won for *Darling*

And then she heard her name called out. In a dream she drifted to the stage to take the golden award. She had no decently prepared speech – though it wouldn't have helped if she had. Her voice was trembling so much she was almost incoherent. Harrison applauded her richly and the crowd went wild. 'I don't know what to say,' she stammered, 'except to thank everyone, especially my darling John Schlesinger for this wonderful film. This is the most wonderful thing on earth. . .' She fled, eyes brimming with tears – finally fully releasing the emotional coil of two years, three major motion pictures, intimate failures, a lifetime's learning. Bessant comforted and congratulated her, unaware at that moment that he had lost her to real stardom. Hollywood had honoured her, and Hollywood would hold her.

Their love affair was as good as over, though neither knew it. Instead they whispered sweet promises about a planned holiday together, reward for their shared labours and patience. Now that *Fahrenheit* was finished there was no work till mid-summer, a chance to idle and perhaps celebrate in their rough-hewn fashion in the Mediterranean sun.

John Schlesinger greeted Christie at Heathrow airport on her return – together with half of Britain's available press fleet. The timing was impeccable. *Zhivago,* having been manhandled to success in the States, was just opening in London and though the critics' previews were glum this new promotional hype was set to see it through: the backers had the extra plug of 'Oscar-winner Christie'.

At Pinewood Truffaut was still meticulously working through *Fahrenheit 451,* scheduled for completion on April 27th, with post-production work that would take it into June. Having seen Christie's footage rough-cut together, unprompted, he praised 'my Miss Julie' to the skies: 'You have two kinds of actors: the poetic and the psychological. Julie is the latter and a pure joy to work with. On top of that her French is so good I may even have to dub her in the film!'

Six months before, returning from Spain after *Zhivago* to find her flat cluttered with bouquets of flowers, Christie had run into a rage and flung the flowers into garbage bins. But now the deluge of unanimous praise from high place washed out her recalcitrance. Drugged by Hollywood, by the fact that she had come through the mangle of bad nerves and tough films, she was at last ready to be garlanded. On her stopover in London before escaping on holiday to Amsterdam and Greece she even returned Hollywood's compliments.

The America she had conditioned herself to hate suddenly turned: 'Hollywood? The greatest place on earth for a holiday. That desert! I had never anticipated anything so beautiful.' But Hollywood filmworld values apparently unsettled her: 'I've got no desire to work in Hollywood. I feel very strongly European.' Shortly after she expanded: 'I can cope with England, I think, whereas America

Osker Werner (left) and Julie Christie meet one of the book people in *Fahrenheit 451*

overwhelms me . . . Somehow Londoners aren't as dazzled by other people's fame as the Americans are. Maybe we're more sophisticated here – or maybe there are simply more famous people living in London! But whatever it is, I adore this place . . . I love its mediocrity, and I mean this in a nice way. Everything in this country works on a fifty percent ratio compared to the all-out one hundred percent coronary-making pace of the States.'

Janni, Schlesinger – everyone with vested interests – breathed easy delight at the subdued, satisfied Julie Christie that returned from the Hollywood Oscars. Whatever doubts her New Year collapse had raised abated; she had exposed herself, everyone surmised, to unnatural pressures in order to prove herself fast. Her future would allow more measured plans, a less hectic existence. Schlesinger prepared *Far from the Madding Crowd* in a mood of high optimism, confident that she might yet win him his own first Oscar.*

That summer was the high-point of her love affair with Bessant – a relaxed, domestic idyll that was over too soon. The Kensington apartment, ironically, never looked prettier – or more like the makings of a permanent family home. Months of desultory do-it-yourself had fashioned a cosy oasis as far from the sterility of star dressing-rooms and top-class hotels as could be imagined. Troops of friends had contributed in their varied talented ways, some building alcove bookshelves, others lovingly restoring the panelled Victorian doors. The original plan to reconstruct the period flavour had been abandoned, but the junk shop bric-a-brac remained – pots and pans of an earlier era, old tin alarm clocks, ancient watercolour prints, antique ornaments. Bogarde's big brass bed dominated one room and the living area was furnished mostly with books accumulated by innumerable mates over several years. There was a shelf television – rarely watched – and a reluctant space for the old Oscar above the old magazine collection just right of the boarded-up fireplace.

During the happy summer Christie mucked about the kitchen, reverting to her lazy old ways. She cooked exotic food, then forgot to eat it. Friends drifted in and out. She smoked a lot – far too much, but cigarettes steadied her nerves – and slept for ten to fourteen hours on end. A few stray cats stopped by for a while, fattened up, then pushed off. Most journalists who phoned were turned away. Rumours that marriage was imminent were scotched by Bessant's friends and one says, 'If ever they were likely to take the plunge it was then. That was a settled time, they were very close.' But Christie held off.

**Darling* was a triple-Oscar winner. The other awards went to Frederic Raphael for Best Screenplay and Julie Harris for Costume Design.

Funnily, perversely, just when things seemed most serene, Christie was itchy for action again. Early in July she told a journalist friend: 'I want to buy a house for about £35,000 with a garden in the right part of London. A marvellous mystery house, all nostalgic and full of memories of the past, with a garden like *The Secret Garden*. That's not to say I don't like the flat I'm in now, though it's in the unfashionable part of London. In fact, I was horrified when an American woman columnist came to interview me and said, "Now that you're a big movie star you'll be moving out to somewhere smart right away?" "Moving out!" I said with as much calm as I could muster. "I'm only just moving in" . . . Besides my flat has the sort of unpretentious atmosphere that I like and lots of little shops all around where I can dash out and buy stuff for a meal at the last minute. Still, if I go on making money on this scale, I'd like to have something to show for it eventually. I'm appalled by the amount of cash I've frittered away on nothings since I had some to spend. . .'

There was no resentment about paying off debts for old, broke mates, but Christie's ideal social set-up altered slightly. For now she was content to share with Bessant and one other chum, a girl called Nickey Croke who worked in the advertising department of a publishing house. Passing friends were still welcome – but on a more temporary basis.

Wealthier than ever that summer, Christie toyed with important purchases. She refused the idea of a Rolls-Royce but thought an American car, something like a Packard, might be fun. In the end, that notion was still-born. A series of driving lessons convinced her she wasn't cut out for motoring. More ambitiously, she planned to invest in art. Art books had replaced histories as her favourite study and she had collected an assortment of good limited-edition prints. The old bruised copies of Hogarth that hung alongside the Bessants on her bedroom wall were no longer enough. She wanted to search out something by Rouault, maybe even something loftier – a Rousseau or Chirico.

When she did start quietly house-hunting she stressed that she wanted somewhere in the city. She was urbanized, she said, and whilst a holiday villa in Spain or Greece might ultimately prove useful, she wanted now to remain at the heart of action, in London. It was with some regret – after a few weeks' break in Holland and Greece with Bessant – that she taxied to the Royal Hotel in Weymouth to commence what would be almost six months shooting on the new Schlesinger. Dorset, like Madrid, at first seemed unbearably remote but this time old familiar faces from previous films were present to offset loneliness. There was cinematographer Nic Roeg whom she'd first met in Spain, and who handled photography on *Fahrenheit;* there was stills photographer Norman Hargood who always seemed to snap

her the way she wanted to be seen; Bubbles Elliott, her stand-in, was always welcome company; even the publicity agents, one American, one British, were old members of what journalists dubbed 'the Christie clan'. Helpful too was the live-in companionship of an old drama school pal, actress Fiona Walker, cast alongside her in a major role. Fiona moved into Christie's hotel suite where, according to reports of the time, she acted as 'maid and confidante'. Later they rented a house together. Bessant, meanwhile, was commuting between jobs in London and Kent, promising to visit whenever he could – most weekends, if at all possible.

Christie was, temporarily, very relaxed and approachable. The cachet of Oscardom seemed to soothe some of the deep self-doubts of recent years and she seemed surer than ever that she belonged to films, and that the course of her career was running well. She had read Thomas Hardy's novel on which the film was based and thought it quite exceptional. Her lead role of Bathsheba, she was in no doubt, was her best yet. Fellow actors who had never worked with her before but knew the legends of her nerviness and slow approach to character build-up approach were surprised to find her calm and keen. She explained that work was everything to her, the Oscar was nice but it didn't mean she was a great actress – she had lots of striving and stretching ahead yet. Dorset and the protective screen of work was a relief for other reasons too. In Holland and Greece, to her appalled surprise, she had become what once she'd claimed she wanted more than anything to be: an instantly recognisible 'face'.

'I specially chose some remote little island,' she groused, 'where no one could possibly recognise me. But no such luck. I was gaped and ogled at by every man I saw, and while women naturally like men to go dotty over them, there was something terribly off-putting about their stares . . . It brought out the worst in me. I wanted to shout at them, and all the time my anger made me feel guilty. It was *awful.*'

The return to Britain and work was like a holiday. 'This sort of heroine-worship doesn't happen as much in London . . . I'm accepted as part of the scenery. Dozens of girls look like me, dress like me and think like me. I have no novelty value at home. If I'm supposed to typify 1966, as some people have claimed, then I'm only one of the many who do.'

The astute and respected film critic Nina Hibbin visited Dorset while shooting was in full swing and reported incisively on the Christie conundrum. The mask of calm, Hibbin judged, concealed all the old weaknesses patched and padded with the fluff of wide celebrity. 'You can't really interview her,' Hibbin wrote. 'Unexpectedly, for an actress riding the full tide of success, she is diffident, unsure of herself, and somehow touchingly vulnerable . . . I asked her how she coped with trying to remain a reasonably balanced person now that she is a

Christie with Don Bessant in 1967

celebrity. Or, rather, I started to ask. Then, sensing her discomfort at being confronted with a direct question, I put forward some of *my own* tentative ideas. . .'

Quite openly she confessed to Hibbin that *Far from the Madding Crowd* was the first film she'd enjoyed working on. Then she speculated anxiously on whether she had enough range and variety of style, and whether the roles she'd taken so far had shown sufficient contrast. Hibbin found herself reassuring Christie, reminding her of the clutch of awards so far, from the Oscar to the new shared Best Actress award from the Moscow Festival. At the same time, in outrageous contradiction, *The Times* sent its man down to interview her and reported on a stable, content superstar. 'I am happy with any good part that comes along,' *The Times* quoted her. 'I don't think anything I've done is like anything else.'

Fahrenheit 451, the movie Christie boldly assessed as her best yet, opened while Schlesinger worked her down in Dorset. On June 21st, wrapping up his diary of the film, Truffaut had marked: 'the end of this adventure in which I have lost quite a lot of hair and gained quite a few white ones.' He was, then, reluctant to probe his achievement: 'I don't know what the film will look like . . . Here, in the case of *Fahrenheit 451,* it was a case of treating a fantasy with familiarity, making out-of-the-ordinary scenes look ordinary and everyday scenes look abnormal. I still don't know whether the film will give the impression of a sane film made by a madman or a mad film made by a sane man. . .'

Overall he, like science-fiction writer Ray Bradbury on whose story the film was based, seemed pleased enough and indeed, on release, some worthy criteria were satisfied. First-rank reviewers in the heavyweight journals were unanimous in praise, and the *Monthly Film Bulletin* concluded: 'There may be other ways of putting Bradbury on film but there can be none better than this.' But *Variety,* while equally glowing, cautioned its cinema renters: 'Cast and director provide needed marquee values for filmization of Bradbury's bizarre peep into the future. Needs careful handling for maximum results.'

As it happened, *Fahrenheit* failed miserably at the box-office and was shown only sparingly in foreign countries – a grave disappointment for Universal, sponsoring a film for the first time from its new London headquarters. Truffaut himself had inadvertently spelled the recipe for disaster when he wondered about the fantasy-familiarity values of the film.

Bradbury's story concerned a totalitarian world of the future where the populace are kept at heel and all books are burnt so that knowledge is restricted (F. 451 is the temperature at which paper burns). Montag (Oskar Werner) is one of the privileged, a fireman who scouts out and destroys books. He is married to the conventional

Linda but falls for her lookalike Clarisse (both roles played by Christie), who encourages him to rebellion. When Linda denounces his wayward traits he turns his flame-thrower on his book-burning colleagues and flees to join Clarisse in the hideout of the 'Book People'.

Dramatically the film is limp and the exposition never quite matches the novelty or promise of the story idea – very much a case of a pint in a gallon pot. Worst of all, many remarked, the fantasy elements of a zombie-ridden futuristic society are not grasped or exploited. Instead, the excitement is lost in heavy moralizing and the picture terminates in appropriate snow-bound depression – Montag on the run, going nowhere, reciting from memory the tales of Edgar Allan Poe. *Variety* thought the treatment lacked verve but found 'no valid grounds for criticising the principal performers . . . Julie Christie is standout.' In the *New Statesman* John Coleman wasn't worried about box-office. For him, 'the result really is something hopeful and affectionate. Nicolas Roeg's superb photography enjoys its environment . . . Truffaut remains a spellbinder.' Coleman's only black mark was scratched against Christie: 'Some doubts linger about Miss Christie's acting ability . . . yet the context absorbs her in both her appearances.'

At the village of Bloxworth in Dorset, assiduously applying herself to Hardy and Schlesinger, Christie kept her head down and ignored the grim rumbles from town. She wanted to talk of the future, not the past. As *Far from the Madding Crowd* progressed she became more involved than ever in the film-making process. A technician says: 'She wasn't a pushy, eager-for-details type but she was interested, she was concerned. Light conditions, weather problems – all the messy troubles of shooting, she made it her business to understand. The crew were her friends. Her caravan was an open house. When it was raining, or cold, everyone was welcome to stop by and join her for a cuppa or a smoke. Her favourite cigs were mentholated and sometimes the caravan was choked with smoke, like a bloody Turkish bath. Her consumption was huge!'

Jo Janni visited often and was impressed with her serious application. He, like Schlesinger, rated *Far from the Madding Crowd* as his most promising movie venture so far. For Schlesinger the appeal was the challenge of translating 'a very special book'; for Janni, for once, there was the pleasure of having no personal investment this time. MGM had underwritten eighty percent of the budget and Janni's share of the fifty-fifty cut of Christie's fee, massively inflated after the Oscar, made up the balance. So Janni and his company stood to lose nothing if the film flopped. All along, however, *Far from the Madding Crowd* gave indications of success – if only *Zhivago*-like success. There were conventional epic elements, Schlesinger agreed, but he was trying for something extra too.

Thomas Hardy's work had only once before been filmed – a silent version of *Tess of the d'Urbervilles* some forty years earlier – but Schlesinger now wanted to 'dig out the dark spiritual side of Hardy . . . with verisimilitude'. The film had not been his choice originally. Janni had proposed it and introduced him to the novel which he loved, and both agreed that Christie was, in real life, the nearest thing to the heroine Bathsheba. In Christie's words she was: 'illogical, vain, proud, but she cares to be good. She has high values and a violent temper; she's vulnerable and eager, but privately resourceful.' The cast was superb – old mates Terence Stamp (who'd been at Central with Christie too), Alan Bates, Peter Finch. The locations were unique, the weather conducive to the required grit-and-grime atmosphere; and yet, halfway through, something started to go wrong.

It would be October '67 before the film opened to public scrutiny but already, Christmas '66, with the last six weeks of shooting in sight, Schlesinger was venting his doubts: 'Its problem has always been not to make it come out as a sort of Reader's Digest of a very long gigantic novel, instead of doing it the justice it deserves. I think we've done it was well as we can.' The wary note of looming failure was unmissable. Christie for her part was too closely involved to be objective. She just kept working, observing the process. But the tone of her dismissive one-liners to the endlessly visiting journalists altered: *Far from the Madding Crowd* was no longer her happiest film, now it was her hardest.

By Christmas the prospect of yet another project must have seemed like yet another welcome escape. Director Richard Lester, riding high with the Beatles' film hits, had offered her a script called *Me and the Arch Kook Petulia,* a pie-eyed modern romance which was to be his first Hollywood film, and she had quickly accepted, swayed suddenly by the notion of an escape ticket to the industry's heartland, the place she'd said she did not want to work – but the place which, all along, many believed had secretly been her end-of-the-rainbow target. Shooting was due to start in late spring, and now she was wishing herself away while, at the same time, refusing to discuss such vagrant thoughts: 'It's months away and not to be thought about. We may all be dead by then.' Certainly she had not lost faith in Schlesinger but as script problems thickened, so too did the weather. The winter was fierce and lovely Dorset became increasingly inhospitable. The film wrapped up, according to publicity lady Catherine O'Brien, 'in the teeth of a biting gale' in mid-February. Christie was, once again, exhausted. But her London homecoming cheered her enormously. The purchase of a new home, a two-storey terraced at 1, Selwood Terrace, South Kensington, had been finalized and Bessant had begun the laborious business of furniture shifting.

Back in Dorset, Schlesinger was brooding darkly over what had

The *Darling* team: Schlesinger (left), Christie and Janni on the set of *Far From The Madding Crowd*

Overleaf: As Bathsheba with Terence Stamp as Sergeant Troy in *Far From The Madding Crowd*

once seemed like the stuff of greater awards, more kudos. He told Catherine O'Brien: 'Now that it's finished I feel that although it's been a very slow process working under such difficult conditions to achieve realism – a tremendous problem – one has gained by having to wrestle with such a monster novel . . . [It] is by far the most difficult job I've tackled in my career, perhaps in some ways the least enjoyable, progressively, as one did it.'

The anticipation of failure, in commercial terms at any rate, was well founded. Hopes for a slow-burning *Zhivago*-type success were quickly dashed. Though the movie was destined to open in the States with the kind of fanfare only afforded to the voguish, the American critics made certain it died a swift though noisy death. The simple old-fashioned story of the Victorian female farmer (Christie) and the three men who vied for her favours was considered slow-paced and boring. In Britain David Shipman admired its 'gentle pleasures amidst the year's blood and violence' and Nina Hibbin found at last a film which lived up in every way to the promise of its source material, the cherished book. Hibbin also concluded, however, that Christie hadn't 'achieved a robust enough spirit for the central role' even though she was surrounded by characterizations of great strength and conviction.

And the *Monthly Film Bulletin*, in a lucid and deeply intellectual piece, believed that 'the interplay between the human and the natural universe is unfortunately lost in the attempt to transfer Hardy to the screen'; Christie's failure, they reckoned, stemmed from her inability to grow with events: 'Bathsheba, as portrayed by Christie, remains extroverted throughout'. Schlesinger made some faint-hearted efforts to defend the work claiming that, after *Darling*, too much had been expected of Christie and himself but the negative critical voice won the day. Sheridan Morley's commentary seemed most darkly foreboding. An admirer of Christie for quite some time, he found the picture 'worthy but somehow uninspiring'. Julie Christie he now saw as 'an erratic gift, sometimes electric, sometimes disappointing'. He noted that she had suffered the heavy onus of bearing the Symbol-of-our-Time tag and still held hope for her, ambivalently recalling the observations of both Kenneth Tynan (who saw her as 'a hockey captain with romantic leanings') and *grande dame* Ingrid Bergman ('she has the most forceful personality of all the young actresses working in films today'). But although *Madding Crowd* was a commercial flop in the U.S., in Britain it fared better. In retrospect, without the inflated epic expectations created by *Zhivago* and its own prepublicity, it emerges as beautifully photographed, smoothly told, and effectively under-stated.

In one fell swoop the critics who had crowned Christie crushed her laurels and made her, overnight, no longer readily bankable. The Oscar idyll became, as so often, a short bitter-sweet honeymoon. This

Previous page: With Peter Finch in *Far From The Madding Crowd*

Far From The Madding Crowd. Alan Bates as Gabriel Oak is in the background

'honourable failure', as screenwriter Frederic Raphael called it, alerted Christie to the transience of film fame and the limitations of working solely within the British industry, confined to pedigree British product. According to colleagues, the shock of *Madding Crowd,* so soon after the intoxicating delights of the Oscar, suddenly determined Christie to widen her horizons. 'It was a period of clear-thinking,' says one. 'The risk of lolling about in the comforts of home celebrity was suddenly obvious and she wanted to expand.' In the circumstances Janni, who might have felt he was losing control of her, was forced to give the Hollywood blessing.

The *Madding Crowd* debacle still lay before her when, in late spring, she followed Dick Lester to Hollywood to try her luck among the so-feared moguls and monster egos. She departed with preconceived notions, mistrustful of America, resolute in her intention to beat the system, to avoid any hollow star harness, to learn and make good.

All that really mattered was a good experience with Lester, a well-crafted and successful end-result. No worry if her cheque was lesser or greater than the MGM pay-out for *Madding Crowd,* no worry if the sour whisper of 'falling star' was already circulating.

She bade Don Bessant a fond adieu, took a houseboat in San Francisco and started to re-establish her faded Grecian tan. She liked Dick Lester and the change to Hollywood was revivifying, as good as the proverbial rest. Her spirits, temporarily deflated again, soared. She regained weight and that impish relaxed-but-resolute smile.

She was looking good when, in the sweltering summer of '67, she met again a man whose path she had briefly crossed at a film reception for *Born Free* the year before. Then she had been fleetingly attracted to him, but he had been no more than a face in a starry crowd. His name was Warren Beatty.

TEMPORARY CINDERELLA?

Warren Beatty, that naive and sentimental lover of so many accomplished lovelies – Natalie Wood, Joan Collins, Leslie Caron (he was named in her divorce from director Peter Hall), Diane Keaton – once definitively outlined his compatibility with Julie Christie when he said: 'To me marriage is essentially a contract and there are so many loopholes in it that Wilbur Mills and the entire Ways and Means Committee at their height couldn't figure it out. I believe that the marriage ceremony is archaic.'

Julie Christie, of similar persuasion, arrived for her first Hollywood working tour still asserting (to Oriana Fallaci): 'I hate myself. I'm so afraid. Afraid of not being liked by other people, of being rebuffed. It doesn't seem logical. I have had very few rebuffs in love, in my career, and yet . . . it is the fear of humiliation as a person, not as an actress, do you see? I'm afraid of being a failure, madly afraid.'

She arrived as Warren Beatty, her lover-to-be and career guide for the next seven years, was scaling the most important pinnacle of his own career. *Bonnie and Clyde,* the movie that would mark a watershed in American cinema, was just completed and Beatty himself was apprehensively watching its first doddering baby steps. The project had been drifting around for years – even Jean-Luc Godard had turned it down – but Beatty (as producer and lead actor) with director Arthur Penn had hammered it into shape at last. Beatty watched with mounting glee through '67–'68 as, by turns, the American critics savaged it, then turned tail while it shattered box-office records and won colossal plaudits from abroad. In one year the film netted nearly $20 million and Beatty was hiked up to the top league of international Hollywood stars, the new *wunderkind.*

On the set of *In Search of Gregory*

Christie herself had stated her attraction to strong successful men, men who could allay her fear of failure, and Beatty's impact on her, at a first casual meeting during the making of *Petulia* (the *Arch Kook* bit

had been dropped) was exceptional, though her integrity and still lively devotion to the absent Bessant must have made it accordingly unsettling. Reports of the time claim Christie and Beatty 'detonated like a match in cordite' and a restrained but passionate association began fairly quickly. There was nothing calculated or decadent about the quick-developing relationship – none of the rake's progress with the innocent abroad. Christie liked Beatty because he was sensitive, successful and adroit in his tracks round the Hollywood jungle she found herself slightly lost in. For him, the attraction was multi-faceted. He had made no bones about the fact that he admired women of achievement and though he was shortly to earn some $6 million personal profits from *Bonnie and Clyde,* she had one up on him with her Oscar. More fairly, he was attracted to her odd blend of pitiless self-honesty and doubt. 'She is almost pathologically honest,' he said. And to add to that: 'She is beautiful by all your conventional standards and I admire her work. So it is no surprise that I love her.'

Love lay ahead. Their first meetings were brief and though Hollywood gossipers fastened on to them swiftly the word was that Christie would dally while *Petulia* ran, then drift back to Bessant, awaiting her at the Fulham house. Beatty for his part might return to his recent lover Leslie Caron.

As the summer progressed the pattern of the relationship became harder to follow. As Beatty toured to promote *Bonnie and Clyde* his staple opening line before a press conference began was often: 'I am *not* going to discuss any of my women or female friends. It's against my principles.'

Christie would neither deny nor confirm any rumours. There was a tacit acceptance that word was out – but that was it. Perhaps, as friends have suggested, she couldn't trust herself to comment because her affections were very confused and, after three years' love, she was naturally loath to offend Bessant. But she did admit to a strengthened affection for America, Hollywood in particular.

The flurry of interest in a blooming Beatty-Christie affair apart, everything was dominated by Lester's tight-packed shooting schedule, virtually entirely on location round the bumpy streets of San Francisco. Pursued by a British press corps freshened by hopes of a scandal Christie would only say that she was loving 'every single minute of San Francisco . . . a wonderful city and everyone here is so friendly and easy-going.' But, she added, thrilling as the experience was, she was homesick. Her thoughts were all about homecoming, building up the new house: 'It'll probably take me years to finish furnishing – it's a long term hobby really. I won't buy super stuff that costs the earth – those prices make me reel back in horror. I go for Victorian junk. Slightly weird. . .'

Petulia, 1968

Home talk was, in truth, a smokescreen – though Christie herself did not yet know it. *Petulia* finished shooting on time, late in the autumn and she flew directly home as planned to prepare *In Search of Gregory,* a first film for established theatre director Peter Wood which Janni was setting up specially for her. Temporarily she was back in Bessant's arms, but the mould of their love affair was irreversibly fractured. Back in Hollywood, Beatty was already scouting, as he promised her he would do, for a film they could star together in, something powerful and special that would potently mix their talents, consolidate their relationship, and win her back to Hollywood for good.

At Selwood Terrace Christie pretended to be unchanged. She still smoke, drank and debated with Bessant's crowd, entertained the odd passing chums, whiled away lazy evenings at the Queen's Elm pub. Irish actor Kevin McHugh recalls: 'Bessant was still her guy – nice bloke, and a fair darts player. But word was out that Beatty had already "happened", that he was going on in the background as it were. Bessant seemed unaffected, but then he wasn't the type of chap who wore his emotions openly, for all to see. No one in the circle spoke about it (the Beatty affair), it was just known.'

The pretence didn't last long, but the end of the love affair was undramatic. Bessant slipped quietly out of Christie's life – still retaining her affection and respect – as *Petulia,* a *tour de force* that displayed consummate acting confidence, went on release.

The magic of Hollywood had worked its trick on yet another Cinderella.

There are those who argue that Beatty's impact on Christie is best assessed by her widely variable performances in her last pictures of the Sixties, *Petulia* and *In Search of Gregory,* the last under the Janni contract. According to Fleet Street gumshoe Nigel Dempster the relationship, in contrast to her association with Bessant, was 'fiery' and she was, apparently, greatly influenced by its ups and downs. *Petulia,* the film that dates from the introductory kiss, was, by consensus, her most mature performance in a very complex part. Aspects of the story reflect *Darling,* particularly in its microcosmic, vaguely mocking, comment on contemporary morality. Christie played 'kooky' Petulia, a faded flower child of the era, married to the forceful and demanding David (Richard Chamberlain) but whimsically attracted to men like Archie (George C. Scott), a divorced doctor with a family.

Despite beatings from David and pressure from his family, Petulia goes her own way, seduces Archie, but still cannot choose a moment to desert her husband and seek a fulfilling better life. Finally, pregnant, Petulia decides the time to quit has come. She agrees to flee with the lovelorn Archie but is thwarted in the end when, as the ultimate decision devolves to him, he shirks and runs.

The strengths of the film were many. Lester's choice of

gimmick-ridden San Francisco as a backdrop vibrantly underscored the difficulties of human communication in a faked-up-wonderland of automation and cheap thrills. The photography by Nic Roeg – soon to direct Christie himself in yet another masterpiece, *Don't Look Now* – was exceptional. But Lester's brave and leapfrog narrative technique was confusing to some. The respected Dilys Powell bemoaned a situation where the critic enlightening the paying public, once he gets past the expository passage outlined above 'is offered nothing but phrases – the kind to which he himself resorts when completely flummoxed – about kaleidoscopic situations, interlaced flashbacks and subliminal imagery.' Still, she had to admit the whole was enjoyable, a success. *Petulia,* she stressed, does not let your mind wander. 'Julie Christie has what might be called the tempo of life for the role. To my mind she is out of place as a purely romantic character' – a side jab at *Madding Crowd's* miscalculation? – 'but in a situation in which, as here, a romantic instinct struggles against a protective covering of smart absurdity she shines.'

Petulia

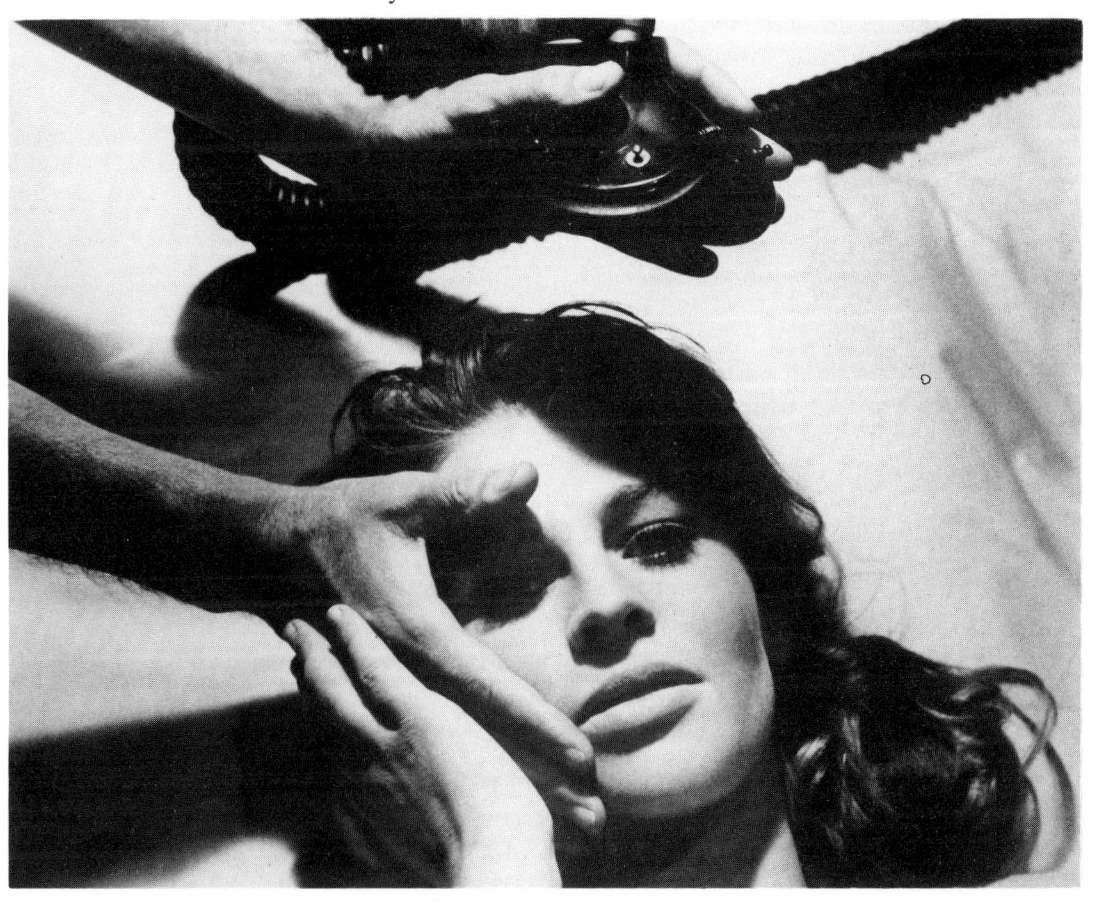

The *Monthly Film Bulletin* politely applauded Lester's first attempt at a serious psychological drama (which Lester himself judged simply 'a sad love story'). For them, Christie's able performance was 'permeated throughout with an insurmountable (apt) sadness'. John Coleman in the *New Statesman* baldly stated: '*Petulia* is Lester's most vulnerable and best film to date. It dares, as his splendid evasive Beatles movies didn't . . . to conduct something more than a flirtation with the human condition.' Once again Christie was keenly praised for her move away from the trammels of Schlesinger-Raphael: 'Miss Christie [is] in her element, which is discotheque rather than Dorset. The freshness of *Petulia,* and the force of it, come rather from a series of extraordinary episodic performances. Julie Christie and George C. Scott . . . are very good.'

In Search of Gregory, another Janni production, shot in Geneva and Milan during the autumn of '68, provided the absolute opposite critical response, fully negative. A muddled, empty film about a girl's (Christie) near nymphomaniacal pursuit of a mystery-fantasy man called Gregory (Michael Sarrazin), it had only a limited circuit release – and even that was much delayed because of the distributors' disenchantment. Patrick Gibbs in the *Daily Telegraph* summed it up, though backhanding some small praise to Christie: 'If *In Search of Gregory* comes out as a silly film it is no doubt because the central character (Christie), who is seldom off screen, is a stupendously silly girl. This need not have counted against the film . . . (but) those concerned don't seem to realize what a silly girl they have on their hands: they take her quite seriously. (But) Christie does all possible with the part.'

Janni must have been disappointed – not only at the nosedive in financial returns but at the growing evidence of Christie's depleted enthusiasm for his British or European-based films, the factor which spelt out the inevitability of their imminent split. While shooting advanced in Geneva he had been telling journalists of his continuing commitment to the star-making process that had launched Christie and, unshakably, to Christie herself. He had two other budding 'stars' on contract – Carol White and Prunella Ransome – but his beloved Julie still occupied most of his thoughts. He had, he explained, shaped her career with the greatest loving care – still did. 'I would spend hours just thinking what sort of film would be right for her. Think, think, think. When I felt I had the right story which is our raw material I would spend thousands of pounds developing it. If it did not seem one hundred percent right it would be scrapped.'

It is hard to know whether *Gregory* ever could have seemed one hundred percent right. Both screenplay and accompanying novel (by Bonnie Golightly) are washy, unappealing documents that evince no great promise. But Christie had her distractions too during the making of the film. As Bessant retreated, so the affair with Beatty blossomed boldly, complicatedly, uncovered, for all the world to see. As the publicity stir round *Bonnie and Clyde* diminished, Beatty had more time to travel and woo. He phoned Christie daily, flew to her side whenever he could. In two years he had turned down some of Hollywood's great roles – leads in *Butch Cassidy and the Sundance Kid* and *Bob & Carol & Ted & Alice* (indeed, he would later turn down the Al Pacino role in Coppola's *The Godfather*) – but now he ventured back before the cameras for a movie largely shot in Europe. His reasons, it was claimed, centred on a desire to be close to Christie, then working in Geneva.

Beatty took over the Sinatra role in *The Only Game in Town* for an unprecedented $750,000, playing opposite Elizabeth Taylor. While shooting in Paris, Beatty entreated Christie to skip off from *Gregory* for a few days to fly and join him – and she readily complied. The writer Robert Ottaway observed her 'fully absorbed in this new relationship . . . watching on the fringes of the set, buying a roll of Indian silk at £50 for a dress and having it remade when Warren didn't like it.'

With co-star John Hurt in *In Search of Gregory*

Beatty was just as besotted. As soon as he could he dashed to Geneva to wine and dine her after her day's work. Now that the secret was out, they paraded together, embraced in public – but still adamantly rejected any private-life revelations. On the set of *Gregory*, as Peter Wood beavered to make the mishmash blend, speculation about a Christie-Beatty merger of some permanent nature was rife. All sorts of fair-weather 'friends' gave 'exclusive' reports about marriage-in-the offing.

But Christie and Beatty would only sourly grimace when more daring journalists chanced the query. Gerard Garrett of the *Evening Standard* studied the evidence and prognosticated shrewdly: marriage wouldn't, couldn't happen but 'what unfortunately strikes a chill in business circles is the widely-held belief that Mr Beatty is thinking of closing the Christie corporation down altogether. Transferring its assets, one could say, from the business to the social sphere. Miss Christie, however, firmly says she is not contemplating going out of business.' Garrett discovered, however, that future film projects hung under a cloud, that no announcements would be made till the absolute last minute because 'any elaborate discussion about Miss Christie's future commitments tends to get Mr Beatty feeling bearish'.

When pointedly asked, Christie just hugged Beatty and said, 'I don't have any plans . . . How do I know what is coming along?'

In fact, as Garrett foresaw, mini-retirement loomed. After *Gregory* Christie repaired to London, then Los Angeles, keeping by Beatty's side. When *Petulia* opened she was only sparsely available for promotion; then, almost literally, she vanished, dipping clear of the film world for eighteen months. With Beatty she toured the world, visiting countries she'd always wanted to see in quick whistle-stops. Then it was back to a double life in L.A. and London. With Bessant gone from the Selwood Terrace house, the place was emptier, less frequently tended to.

Domestics Unlimited, an enterprising housekeeping and cleaning agency which was the bread and butter of so many out-of-work young actors and minor directors, assumed the daily duties. Assigned to dust the drapes and make Christie's bed was a young writer-director, now a BBC veteran. He remembers: 'A big, spare house with an ornate old-world toilet that belonged in an exhibition somewhere; the brass bed was in the basement room . . . Christie wasn't always around and the place was often unlived in. She was quite casual about things like possessions and tidiness but she kept a collection of cherished photo albums and did like to see a job well done.'

She was also generous. The once-a-fortnight cleaning fee was £2, payable directly to whoever executed the task. Possibly with an eye on her tax allowance situation, under sway of her advisers, Christie always paid by cheque, 'a novelty' to the cleaner. 'But it was always

As Catherine in *In Search of Gregory*

£2. 10s – no comment about it, no big deal. I think she just probably felt for those in her profession who lived on the other side of success. She was matter-of-fact and didn't converse or sympathize openly, but she was . . . decent.'

Many of the suggested explanations of her retirement from films were unfair or, simply, untrue. Disillusion with Janni's six years of control could not be a factor. After all, his programme had brought her an Oscar, which gave her *Petulia,* Hollywood and autonomy. She had affection and admiration for Janni, as much perhaps as for Schlesinger; but she had earned her freedom from pressing contracts and deadlines and, understandably, welcomed a period of no commitments. Similarly, she had not tired of films *per se*. She enjoyed going to movies and preferred novel-reading to daily newspapers, frequently wondering how individual books might translate to screen, teasing out the issue with friends. While Beatty determinedly searched for that 'ideal project' to co-feature them she constantly looked over his shoulder, a very interested party. She watched as he developed a script which was to become *Shampoo,* with writer Robert Towne, and provided opinion and encouragement.

There were those, too, who believed she had retired because she was bored with the exposure of celebrity and had enough money anyway. In '65 a seven-year projection of her earnings, arrived at by agents and her solicitor, was £475,000 – a conservative estimate. But in Geneva for *Gregory* she was lamenting her poverty. She took a fancy to a castle that towered over Lake Geneva and jocularly told visitors, 'I'd like to know the man who owns that house!' As indeed might a lot of people: his name was Rothschild. 'I shall never be rich,' she expanded, 'because I hate money. Its only use is to live and do good around you. What pleasure is there shutting it up in a bank? I never have any (money) . . . It's not good to earn too much.'

Inevitably there were those who mocked her selfless assertions: what did she need to earn more for? Beatty was already a millionaire many times over. Yet when Christie moved to L.A. to be near Beatty, once the quick world tour was over, she remained surprisingly independent. He was scouting for a house but kept his luxury roof-top bachelor suite at the Beverly Wiltshire Hotel, one of the swishest in the world. She opted to live separately, renting Gayle Hunnicutt's little beach house at Malibu, right on the ocean's edge. 'Our paths didn't cross, we moved in quite different social circles,' Gayle Hunnicutt says, 'but I take it she was happy in Malibu and she liked the house – and, evidently, her strange arrangement with Warren.'

In reality, her reasons for quitting had to do with indulging the luxury of new love, and a kind of post-success hangover. She had worked her butt off for Janni through the sixties, had finally succeeded in Hollywood and was savouring the chance to briefly catch her breath.

She was also savouring Beatty and subjugating herself to some extent to his career plans. It was a time for talking shop and taking stock and she trusted him to find her the right next big project.

Life with Beatty was not as dreamy as the popular press first supposed. Both were strongly-opinionated, independent, sexually-charged people, differing mostly in their attitude to their own fame. Beatty appeared unaffected by his infamous 'Meaty Beatty' tag and often taunted the press with remarks like: 'In my relations with women I have lived by one motto and one motto alone. That is: prudence. He who lives by the sword, shall die by the sword!' Christie, on the other hand, wanted to put the dip-lipped Diana persona behind her. She told friends she was sick of daily street recognition and had begun to 'feel like Lassie the Wonder Dog'. In England she had even changed her regular pub, in order to avoid the usual boorish encounters.

A journalist says, 'She had become quite neurotic about being Julie Christie – to add to her existing neuroses. There was great ambiguity. She wanted to be talented, to be seen to be talented and special. But she did not want to be Julie Christie. I think the relationship with Beatty was valuable to her because he became her covering screen: he

With Adolfo Celi in *In Search of Gregory*

was bigger and richer than her and she paled to insignificance beside him.'

The writer Robert Ottaway believed on the contrary that 'her relationship with Beatty reinforced her own fear of being swallowed up by her own myth' – primarily because she could observe at close hand the pressures of fame working on someone else. The relationship was, undeniably, charged with some tension. Ottaway wrote politely of her neurotic behaviour, a possible legacy of years of relentless exposure and pressures. She was 'impulsive to a fault, domestically disorganized, needing firm handling'. She even needed friends 'to take her shopping when stocks . . . ran low'. But she was still stout-hearted, a fighter, and she fought with Beatty.

The man from Domestics Unlimited recalls one tiff, during a stopover in London: 'There was I, poised between them, making up the bed, lips sealed, while this furious row raged. I can't remember what it was about. I didn't want to know. I just recall feeling how absolutely farcical the situation was. And Julie *could* shout!'

Christie complained to associates: 'Warren doesn't drink, doesn't smoke, doesn't swear. That makes it a bit hard on me – because I can't do any of those things with him either!' Beatty's friends, for their part, were amazed that his 'old fashioned notions' about wanting to be the breadwinner in this instance accommodated his fondly-held plan to find a co-starring film venture. He was not, obviously, intimidated by Christie or her talent as rumour suggested he had been of other lovers. On the contrary, her talents were a challenge.

Late in '69 Beatty found the script that fitted his hopes for Christie's reawakening. It was based on a grim and offbeat comedy novel called *McCabe* by Edmund Naughton and had been developed as *The Presbyterian Church Wager* by M*A*S*H* director Robert Altman and friend Brian McKay. Negotiations for financing with Warner Bros began and suddenly, in the midst of fervid deal-making, Christie decided she wanted to work again – quickly. *McCabe* would be ready to roll at the start of '71 at the earliest, so there was time to snick in something extra. Maybe, before nailing her colours to Beatty's mast, in the hiatus after Janni, she wanted this one opportunity to freelance. She hurried through a pile of submitted scripts and rejected many. Then producers Norman Priggen and John Heyman offered her a Harold Pinter screenplay, adapted from L.P. Hartley's classic period novel, *The Go-Between*. 'She was,' the producers later confessed, 'a little lukewarm to begin with. But after reading the first five pages she said, in effect, "This is the part I *must* play".'

She flew to England with Beatty's blessing and weeks later he joined her, on location with director Joseph Losey in Norfolk. She rented a house near the sea and purchased a bicycle to take her to the set each day. The fan cavalcade, doubled by Beatty's presence and redoubled by the mystery of her recent retreat from cinema screens, made life hell for a while. The location was besieged like never before, telephoto lenses clicking into focus over every hedge and farm gate. The film's publicists, ever sensitive to real-life drama, had a field day: 'Julie tries her hardest to accept that success means inconvenience. That means battalions of admirers following her around . . . She tries, yes. But she'll openly admit it is all a great burden and honestly she'd rather do without it. You could say she is a girl in a whirl of torment. *That* is why she is so seldom seen on screen. . .'

The film was a happy one and Losey and Pinter, like co-lead Alan Bates, openly adored Christie. Her occasional flare-ups, usually directed at herself – or at too-intrusive reporters – were instantly defended by Bates in particular. Losey considered her special, much enriched by her Hollywood experience. For him she was 'the *only* actress who could play this part.' He elaborated gushingly: 'I can't say enough good things about her. . .' and agreed with Bates that 'a great artiste is entitled to some temperament.'

The greatest cause of anger for Christie was the too-often repeated question: was she likely to marry Beatty? Sometimes, when asked once too often, she would curse, turn heel and stomp away. Her old declaration of independence was unendingly invoked: 'Most men don't relish responsibility., Neither do I.' *Screen* magazine, among others, stubbornly refused to be deterred: 'Close friends say Julie is beginning to reconsider. They believe that she and Warren will probably marry within six months because Julie has always said (sic) "I want to have a child by the time I'm thirty." She is twenty-nine now.'

Christie's clear influence on Beatty's routinely flash lifestyle was generally seen as a promising sign. During a break in filming the couple visited a nearby pig farm where the process of animal slaughter horrified Christie. Within twenty-four hours she declared herself from henceforth vegetarian. 'It was so appalling,' she told everyone and anyone who would listen. 'I couldn't believe that that was what was meant by "factory" farming. Animals were being kept in a concentration camp.' Beatty, to everyone's amazement, backed her up: the procedures were shocking, he would never eat meat again. This impassioned solidarity was seen as a sure sign of paving the way for a legalized bond.

But the truth of it was, shamelessly, at twenty-nine, Julie Christie was still in flux, as unsure of the future as she was doubtful of many achievements of the past. Warren Beatty, and her producers, shared the rewards and the risks of that constant inner conflict.

Exactly as *Screen* was vociferously predicting imminent marriage, others were anticipating separation. It was, they said, highly unlikely that the romance would survive the making of *McCabe*.

HITS AMID BREAKAGES

The tense predictions of a master movie in the making with *The Go-Between* represented no more than high hopes. Losey saw it, in simplest terms, as romantic melodrama: 'if you like, a gentler version of *Lady Chatterly's Lover,* if you leave out the complexities of the time relationship' (the narrative leaps forward sixty years from time to time). But Christie's return automatically elevated aims and expectations. The year before Schlesinger had said of her: 'She is a marvellously instinctive girl. I think though she'd be first to admit she is not technically perfect.' It was generally felt now that her time in Hollywood had broadened her technical sense and she was better equipped than ever for a part like the love-hungry Marian, a part not greatly different from, say, Bathsheba of *Madding Crowd.*

Most of the filming took place at Melton Constable Hall, a huge, elegant, derelict house twenty miles from Norwich which originally belonged to the Astley family who, in the eighteenth century, had been granted the barony of Hastings. Subsequently the Duke of Westminster acquired the property and movie star Madeleine Carroll lived there in the twenties with her husband Captain Philip Astley, nephew of the twenty-first Lord Hastings. Losey borrowed the house from the current owner, a farmer, and completely refurbished it at colossal cost.

Christie's role of Marian was one corner of an intriguing triangular relationship, with Alan Bates as Ted, the man she secretly loved, and newcomer Dominic Guard as their twelve-year-old messenger, the 'go-between'. Marian is forced to engage in a covert relationship with Ted because she is aristocracy and he a mere tenant farmer, frowned upon by her family. In the end, despite their superficial affections, the boy betrays Marian and scandalizes the lovers, causing Ted to commit suicide; in a sensitive epilogue, some sixty years later, the go-between visits Marian, now married and widowed and is asked once again to act

In Joseph Losey's *The Go-Between*

a messenger in an attempt to reconcile her with her grandson who resembles Ted.

When the movie wrapped, Losey was confident he had accomplished something worthwhile. Early previews from visiting critics were good but MGM, the American backers, disliked the end result so much they instantly offloaded, selling cheaply to Columbia who reluctantly pushed it out without much enthusiasm in the autumn of '71. As ever, in the way of the crazy ironies of the film business, MGM was destined to regret its speedy decision. After taking a Grand Prix at Cannes, *The Go-Between* rocketed off to excellent notices and good consistent international business. George Melly in *The Observer* celebrated a film 'architecturally as solid as the great house' itself. He,

Offset on *The Go-Between*

Opposite: An Edwardian bathing belle in *The Go-Between*

BCC

like all major critics, welcomed the ultimate realization of the Losey-Pinter partnership already tried but only half-tested with *The Servant* (1963) and *Accident* (1967). For him, as for others, Christie's homecoming performance was perfect. 'I've seen it three times,' Melly concluded, 'on each occasion with increased pleasure and respect.'

The busman's holiday in Britain on *The Go-Between* started speculation that Christie was about to return to the Schlesinger camp for further important movies. Badgered by reporters, she simply shrugged and said she was unsure of the future. One positive project was offered: $400,000 to play *Camille* in a remake of the Garbo classic. Christie, allegedly advised by Beatty, rejected. *Photoplay* fastened on the enigmatic, self-effacing link with the former *Camille* star: 'Certainly Julie is getting much like Garbo in her attitude . . . She prefers to be left alone.'

Friends at that time comprised a small, unbreachable group that floated around the Malibu beach house and kept themselves to themselves. One colleague stated: 'Julie has all she wants in Warren. He is her new mentor and father and mate. Her other friends drift in and out, but there's no one really close.' After *The Go-Between* Christie fled into the blanketing bosom of her friends and was, for press and public, again unreachable. 'Her lifestyle was strange, to say the least,' says a leading American actress. 'What went on at the beach house was a closely-protected private world. Her main occupation seemed to be making little glass ornaments for presents for her friends . . . you'd see them all over the place.'

There was contentment for Christie – 'the Pacific is like a great comforting mother' – but a fair share of angry disorder too. Gayle Hunnicutt occasionally received little notes informing her pithily of breakages – items of furniture damaged beyond repair. And the gossip columnists were forever hinting at escalations of war between the lovers, and all sorts of troubles that might jeopardize the upcoming *McCabe and Mrs Miller* – the renamed *Presbyterian Church Wager,* to be directed by Robert Altman in the New Year.

As it happened *McCabe,* shot on location in Vancouver, Canada, turned out to be one of Christie's smoothest film experiences and, in retrospect, her best to date. It was unlike anything she had done before, a film pervaded with myriad characters rambling in half-private reveries, suffused by the sombre tones of the elements in chaos, depressingly light-hearted, happily grim, anarchic, naturalistic to the point of being anti-entertainment, anti-film: a classic Robert Altman movie.

Beatty underplayed exquisitely as down-and-out McCabe who arrives in the squalid northwest mining town of Presbyterian Church and, on a lucky streak, wins enough money to open a tented brothel with jaded tarts. Into his dumb life stalks the brash and viper-tongued

Previous page: Offset on *The Go-Between* with Alan Bates

As Constance Miller, the bordello madame, in *McCabe and Mrs Miller*

Mrs Miller (Christie, with an edge to her as never seen on screen before), to rattle him into the notion of a proper lavish bordello with frilly whores and good growth potential. McCabe himself becomes a client of Mrs Miller in the new arrangement but oversteps himself and eventually gets killed in an inter-town dispute, attempting to defend his prospering business. His demise goes unseen by Mrs Miller, who retreats to an opium den while the climactic snowbound shoot-out occurs.

McCabe and Mrs Miller was significant as Altman's return, after brief deviation, to a *M*A*S*H*-like exploration of human absurdities. His story device – a stark comment on the growth of capitalism – was exceptional in its simplicity and perfectly-paced in a

With Warren Beatty in *McCabe and Mrs Miller*

very original execution. Everyone involved received good notices and Christie won the finest of her career from Charles Champlin in the *Los Angeles Times:* 'Miss Christie, hair done up in a cheap frizzle, gives one of the best performances of her career, creating a character who is tough and cautious and too aware of the cruelties and costs of the real world to be your traditional harlot with the heart of gold. There's tenderness there, or a brusque affection, but it's guarded by years of scar tissue. The charm of her playing is that she lets us see the sensitivity which the character has to conceal.'

Christie had always fondly expressed a hope to appear in a cowboy film and she was 'proud of her first Western' and undoubtedly grateful

A promotional cartoon from *McCabe and Mrs Miller*

to Beatty and Altman. The long shoot in hostile country had not, as many promised, destroyed the Beatty-Christie merger. But, despite her gratitude, it did nothing to advance the affair any further either.

By the time *McCabe* was ready for release, late in '71, Beatty was in Europe, making *The Heist* for Richard Brooks, with Goldie Hawn. Christie kept him company most of the time, but based herself stoutly in London, at Selwood Terrace. Allegedly there was strain. Gossipers once again joyously recounted rows and tantrums that seemed to stress their incompatiblity. Even Altman had observed that both functioned differently in public: 'She used to sit on the edge of those [star] parties, while Warren mingled.'

When they returned to Hollywood to the tickertape fanfare of *McCabe's* success Beatty was said to have proposed marriage to Christie, but she refused him. A film writer says: 'They were the show-couple of the seventies, John and Yoko of the film world. Only thing was, they liked to crusade in private so the gossip-mongers had a field day, guessing at what went on behind closed doors. Word had it that Beatty wasn't able to handle her, that he was turned down on the marriage offer. She, apparently, enlightened him, political animal that he was, about the politics of the radical left. She'd been brought up with conservative values, she said, but she always voted socialist. And that was a new area of interest for her – society reform and politics.' The same noted writer recalls: 'The bottom-line speculation. One story had it that Julie got quite fed up with Beatty's vanity. He was supposed to hog the bathroom for hours on end while she paced about in frustration outside, waiting while he crimped and curled his pubic hair.'

While talk of declining relations buffeted round, Beatty was defiantly loyal. He announced for the world, apropos of *McCabe*: 'She is one of the great actresses in the history of films.' And at last he would comment about the intensity of their love: 'If ever we split up, I'll pay her alimony – that's if she wants or needs it.'

A few months later he was squiring Norwegian actress Liv Ullmann round the Hollywood hotspots and Christie was out of 'retirement' again, this time winging to Venice to join old pal Nic Roeg on his new venture, directing a Daphne du Maurier occult thriller.

Early in March the *Daily Mirror* reported: 'It doesn't look as though Julie Christie is going to take up that offer of alimony.' Beatty made no attempt to follow Christie to Venice and the buzz of rumour was soon confirmed: a chapter, maybe the most important and career-shaping relationship in her life, was closed. Questioned heatedly she would only say: 'I don't suppose I've done more than half a dozen films in the last ten years and I know that's not many for an actress.' The inference, widely understood, was that distractions of romance had cramped her career.

The uncom-promising Mrs Miller

Many supposed a new super-active era would begin, a career reconstruction programme fired with all the nervous energy of the sixties. They were wrong. Julie Christie had acquired fresh interests – the joy in privacy; of studying earnestly, especially histories. And anyway, the spell of Warren Beatty, sometimes distracting, always demanding, still lingered.

At the low ebb of the breakdown with Beatty, Christie could easily have crashed on Roeg's ambitious film, only his second as director, *Don't Look Now.* With any other director, conceivably she might have. But Roeg is nothing if not assertive in his demands: he simply did not permit her to waver. Co-star Donald Sutherland's experience demonstrates Roeg's unambiguous and, in this instance, felicitous approach:

> 'I phoned Nic Roeg from Florida after I had read the script of *Don't Look Now* and said that I wanted to sit down and talk to him about it. He said: "What do you want to talk about?" I replied with this long speech about how I felt that ESP was a positive part of our lives and therefore we should make *Don't Look Now* a more educative sort of film, that the characters should in some way benefit from ESP and not just be destroyed by it. Nic said: "That's not how I feel." I said, "Well what do you feel?" and he just said: "What's in the script, do you want to do it or not?" I asked if we could talk about it and he said "No". So I said, "Well if you want to put it that way, yes I do. . ." and I just went and obeyed orders and had a wonderful time.'

Roeg's filmic vision was always, as Sutherland quickly learnt, that it's not a star's job to create a character but to understand what character the *director* wants to create. Unlike theatre, where the actor engages and communicates directly with his audience, the film experience is relayed through a director's lens – so he must be the final arbiter of choice.

Christie was fortunate to land a part with such a director at this time. *Don't Look Now,* despite the gloom of the break-up that surrounded it, turned into a good experience – and a powerful, fully-crafted success to rank alongside *McCabe.* In subject matter, and the character she played, it could not have been more different.

Don't Look Now tells of John and Laura Baxter (Sutherland and Christie) who have lost their young daughter in a drowning accident. Recovering from the horror they move to Venice where John has a work assignment and there encounter two elderly psychics who claim to 'see' the daughter. Impressionable Laura is elated but John's rationalism is affronted. The sisters eventually warn Laura that John's

As Laura Baxter in Nicholas Roeg's *Don't Look Now*

life is in danger, but he ignores the threat and the implications of fleeting glimpses of a red-clad figure, in the distance like his daughter, which he sees in the Venice alleyways. When Laura is summoned to England with news that their other child is ill, John finds himself haunted by *her* continuing presence. Finally he catches up with one 'ghostly' apparition – the red-clad figure – which turns out to be a murderous very real-life dwarf. As the signs foretold, John is killed, knifed to death.

Reviewer Penelope Houston identified Roeg's special theme: a man in some way willing his own death – for her 'the inevitable culmination' of ideas in his two earlier films, *Performance* (1972 co-directed with Donald Cammell) and *Walkabout* (1972). She praised the colour usage, the imagery, the hocus-pocus story tricks; but the brilliance was not all achieved by camera wizardry: 'All the leading performances are striking.'

For both lead actors the film had its trials. Sutherland found that Roeg's fascination with death wishes, a controlled obsession in frequent later films, filtered into his own psyche. 'The experience was like living right on the edge of everything . . . We shot the climax last and I knew I was going to die in it and I became literally convinced that I would die, and dying began to feel almost like a sexual rite.'

Christie's trauma was less intense but, for the moment, no less unnerving. Since *Darling* she had always bluntly insisted she would never again strip off for a role – in *no* circumstances could she imagine it, in the hard-worn old cliche, 'essential for the plot'. (The nude scene in *Darling* had been cut in America, obviously not to the detriment of the film's impact.) Now, with Roeg, she faced the same directorial entreaties, though this time more emphatically: Roeg wanted her to strip for a detailed intimate love-making scene with Sutherland. The six-minute non-stop nude scene, to be filmed 'behind closed doors in a locked studio in Venice', had not originally appeared in the final draft of the shooting script. But halfway through the film Roeg decided some expression of well-balanced marital love should be explicitly shown.

In his grasshopper way he expands: 'I wanted to get a sense of the man and woman married, a loving relationship . . . not fucking, but loving . . . I mean, there comes a point in a relationship, men-men, women-women, men-women, dogs and women! . . . when you appreciate each other. And I didn't want them to show an *ambience*, because it's a *bond* thing. I thought Donald and Julie, in terms of all the rest of the movie, they were incredible. But they never hold hands . . . I just felt they needed a tender something. In fact, in the broadest sense I wanted to feel that there was going to be a progression of life . . . They had lost a child . . . and I wanted the sense that they would have another.'

On location in Venice with co-star Donald Sutherland in *Don't Look Now*

Christie, in no mood for protracted haggling, finally acceded to Roeg's requests and did the scene. In contrast to *Darling* eight years before, the resultant rumpus was sudden and furious. The film was notorious even before its release and was instantly banned sight unseen in a few American Midwest towns. The American censors eventually insisted on clean-up cuts, requesting that *nine frames,* presumably showing sexual organs clearly, be removed. Roeg finds this laughable: 'He (the American censor) examined the film frame by frame . . . And actually on finding nine frames in different spots – that's less than a flick of the fingers – asked for cuts. And we extracted those nine frames and it didn't make any difference at all. You can't tell! *Nine* frames! It's sixteen frames per foot of film, twenty-four to the second – so can you imagine *nine* frames?'

In Britain Stephen Murphy, the censor, passed the film uncut while Mr Stewart Stevens, secretary of the Festival of Light condemned: 'If it's too hot for America where almost anything gets shown it's not difficult to imagine how explicit it is!' Further protests, he pledged, would be made. Donald Sutherland, who like Christie found the scene no more or less than awkward to do, defended the full version: 'The censorship in England is terrific. They thought the scene was one of the most beautiful they had seen . . . The scene is fundamental to the film and takes it from something else into a love story. Take it out, and the film loses a whole dimension.' Jack Worrow, spokesman for distributors British Lion, announced in a left-footed attempt to clarify runaway rumours that hinted the love-making had been for real: 'Julie Christie and Donald Sutherland were both unclothed during the scene. They are making love and their bodies are entwined, so you see some bottoms and bosoms but no full frontals. The scene is done with sincerity and skill. British Lion does not consider it "near the knuckle" and clearly neither does the censor.'

Curiously, for some, Christie on screen nude at thirty looked unerotic, wonderously vulnerable. Alongside willowy Sutherland she looked puny and fragile, most accurately portraying her true tiny self – 5′ 3″, just eight stone, and lean limbed. 'I think,' says film writer Tony Crawley, 'she probably enjoyed it, elements of the recklessness of middle age maybe? She felt, dammit: you want to see? – then this is me. It wasn't half measures. It was complete nudity, complete revelation.' Did it have something to do with sloughing off Beatty? 'Unlikely. Probably it had everything to do with throwing off an image, though. The sixties doll-image still haunted her but in *Don't Look Now* she was Missus Average, urban housewife with kids and problems and an ordinary, unabashed love life.'

Frederic Raphael, image-making writer, believes: 'Thanks to a certain snobbishness she has always chosen to be in classy rather than glossy pictures. Only in *Don't Look Now* did gloss and class work

Overleaf: In *Shampoo,* Warren Beatty's 1975 success as both producer and star together.' Probing for that extra dimension in the work he finds that 'consistent element' of all her films: 'She has not the serenity nor the complacency of the established diva. Those who look for the consistent element . . . will not have missed that she plays a woman cruelly *damaged* by the death of her child for which *she feels* responsible.' He develops his argument: 'If Julie symbolizes the independent modern woman, contemptuous of convention and wary of commitments, she has posed a problem she has never solved, that of how to live at peace with herself.'

As Raphael noted, despite reasonable hits with movies like *The Go-Between* and *McCabe,* Christie's bankability status was no longer impressive. Still sought after, she was not in demand. It was unlikely too that the hat trick completed by *Don't Look Now* would immediately improve the situation. 'She was her own worst enemy,' an actress colleague summarizes. 'She didn't wish to pay her dues to the Star System and she didn't want to flit from trash to trash just because a funded project was conveniently on offer. Her other problem, it seems, was her own uncertainty about herself and who she wanted to be, or what she wanted to be doing.'

Though, by turns, she had said she'd lost interest in theatre, then pined for it, out of the blue she accepted a theatrical role, playing in Chekov's *Uncle Vanya* on Broadway not long after the release of Roeg's film. The production was a short run flop and Christie's performance, in the eyes of Pauline Kael, was 'a vacuum'. Deflated, she returned to L.A. to resume old friendships, even see Beatty again. 'The evidence,' Tony Crawley suggests, 'is that the affair, despite the set-back around *Don't Look Now,* had never really ended. It lasted some seven years, apparently ending in July '74 when he wandered off in the direction of Carrie Fisher.'

Certainly, right through to the spring of '74 and Beatty's preparation for his biggest movie venture since *Bonnie and Clyde – Shampoo,* a satirical comedy which he'd been six years honing – a lively contact was maintained. They talked regularly on the telephone, dined together, were even rumoured in Hollywood columns to be reassessing marriage.

During the summer of '74 director Hal Ashby (Beatty's umpteenth choice: several directors had turned him down) put *Shampoo* into production and Christie was centrally cast, perhaps not coincidentally, as macho stud Beatty's ex-girlfriend. Weeks after the film finished another split occurred when Christie, in Nigel Dempster's words, 'went off with an American industrialist'. It was the first time anyone had walked out definitively on Warren Beatty. But was it to be so clear cut? Reeling from the rigours of *Shampoo* and his foundering marathon affair, Beatty stumbled into the arms of Michelle Phillips, former wife of John Phillips, her partner in singing group the Mamas

and Papas. (Michelle's second husband was actor Dennis Hopper; their marriage represented some kind of Hollywood record, lasting all of eight days.)

By February '75 and the premiere of *Shampoo* talk of a Beatty-Phillips union was hot and frequent. At last Beatty had found the house he was looking for – the one he'd intended to share with Christie. It was the former home of opera singer Lauritz Melchior, a $5 million four-and-a-half acre aerie above Beverly Hills, and he promptly installed Michelle here (along with her daughter, China, by Phillips) but stayed himself in his ill-kempt Beverly Wiltshire penthouse, affecting a continued bachelor life. Christie, meanwhile, was living up the Pacific Highway at Malibu alone and 'rather depressed', according to Fleet Street. But the split seemed final enough and, although some amicable contact was kept up, no real effort was made to re-start an affair.

In April when Beatty flew to London to attend *Shampoo*'s premiere Michelle kept him company but, sensitive to his locale perhaps, he pushed her into the background. She protested: 'He doesn't want anyone to know I'm here.' In May, inevitably, Michelle was gone, replaced by yet another talented beauty, the Russian actress Viktoria Fyodorova. If Christie was offended – even dazzled – by his speedy reorganization of home affairs, she kept it strictly to herself. After *Shampoo* she resumed a reclusive life at Malibu and turned down successive tawdry scripts of the sexy-satire *Shampoo* type.

On August 27th in his *Mail* Diary Nigel Dempster described again a reunion in 'the enduring romance' of Christie and Beatty. Beatty arrived on business leaving Michelle (apparently briefly back on the scene) at his Mulholland Drive hilltop home. On Monday August 25th he took Julie for 'an intimate dinner at Leith's', a noted gourmet restaurant in Notting Hill. Said Dempster: 'Refusing a secluded spot in an alcove, Warren, dressed all in white, instead placed himself at the most visible table, which has a spotlight directly above it. Alas, the evening seemed to follow the established pattern of their relationship. They appeared to be conducting a dignified row as they ate their way through salmon and veal and drank red wine. By the time they left – Julie was dressed in her usual gipsy clothes and shawl – the conversation had become less heated and their chauffeur-driven car took them home.' Dempster also noted that Beatty was no stranger to Christie's neighbours. 'When he wasn't living with her he could be observed every morning in her garden, doing his calisthenics.'

Returning to Hollywood, Christie went back to the comfort of her Pacific retreat and Beatty to Phillips. When asked about his tardiness in taking the plunge he replied wryly that he may well yet do it: 'The best time for a wedding is noon. Then if things don't work out, you haven't blown the whole day.'

Warren Beatty in the background in *Shampoo*

A year later he was in love with Diane Keaton and Christie was less in love with everything. There were no fresh movie plans, even though *Shampoo* was pulling a fortune at the box-office. And America, suddenly, wasn't quite right. 'I loved America but I was resentful of America. I remember all the time I kept protesting: I don't *live* here, I'm only passing through. I couldn't believe they were wasting so much. Throw away, throw away.' In the freewheeling time that had allowed much reading and self-education she had refined a new set of values, an interest in ecology that was soon to play a vital part in her life. 'Do they think all that plastic just disappears? The food, the electricity, that waste is just unbelievable for a European to see. . .'

America, darling America, the beautiful desert, lost its hold on her; just as Beatty had, just as Schlesinger and Janni had . . . She ambled back to England, like dreamy Lizzie in *Billy Liar,* kicking one heaven for another.

BACK IN SITU

But first there was *Shampoo*, like a glorious coda at the end of a dizzying melody. A comedy of sexual manners, in which Beatty as trendy Hollywood hairdresser George goes on a penis-dunking rampage for no notable purpose beyond the obvious seemed to some just a comic, encapsulated replay of Life with the Lion, as seen through the eyes of the sympathetically involved. George has his fun, the girls have their fun – but in the end he loses the one he wants, Jackie, played by Julie Christie. In spite of his casual flings with just about every girl on screen it's to Christie alone he announces: 'You're the only one I can trust. . .'

The outspoken raunchiness of the movie attracted huge audiences and the real-life parallels, as widely reported, hiked ticket sales. Stanley Kaufman in the *New Republic* was outraged, finding the film 'disgusting – fake porno of the most revolting kind. If Beatty and Christie had the guts to *do it*' – close-ups and well-lighted shots of their couplings – 'it might have shaken our whole topography of fantasy and reality.' Which, in essence, said to many: come and play voyeur on Hollywood's former top couple. Though Christie's response to such reaction isn't on record, it's clear she knew from the script what she was letting herself in for. Beatty for his part was unrepentant. As Tony Crawley deduced, he seemed keener to protect rather than exalt his image. He told *People* magazine: 'I wanted to challenge the assumption that a hypersexual character with women, a Don Juan, is misogynist or a latent homosexual. As for comparisons between George and me, I'm not offended by them.' For the rest, he shrouded analysis of the film in references to its peripheral political content.

Adverse reaction to *Shampoo* helped its success enormously. The U.S. Catholic Conference gave it a C rating – morally objectionable in toto for Roman Catholics, the severest of the Conference's six

Shampoo

categories. The Conference deemed the film 'one of the most disappointing in recent history' but conceded that the cast was 'beautiful to watch even though they go through some of the ugliest situations . . . outside of hardcore theatres.' Alexander Walker saw similarities with *Darling* ('a demeaning scramble for wordly wealth and success' – on George's behalf this time) but had only passing regard for Christie. Some personal redemption, however, came from fussy Pauline Kael who had only recently damned *Uncle Vanya*. For her, Christie's 'lived-in, libidinous face' had never been 'harder, more petulant, or more magical. Jackie is coarse and high-strung, a true L.A. combo; she's a self-destructive winner and Christie plays her boldly with a moody ruthlessness I find uncanny.'

If *Shampoo* was some miniaturized re-enactment of a crippled affair in which, coyly, Beatty and Christie played overblown caricatures of themselves then its subtly inconclusive ending, pointed up by the juxtaposition of sunny optimistic Beach Boys music with Jackie's desertion of George, was properly accurate. The Beatty-Christie love

With Goldie Hawn in *Shampoo*

was over for good, but warm affection remained and the couple would soon act together again in Beatty's first pitch as director, *Heaven Can Wait*.

'The Beach Boys come up very quickly at the end,' Beatty stated, 'which I had always hoped would show most people that we were not going into some funeral dirge. There's no doubt in my mind that in two hours George has got his address book out and is thumbing through the numbers . . . and Jackie takes on a series of young lovers.' In other words, they love and lose – and survive.

Julie Christie had a rigid 'no comment' for the press on her *Shampoo* work. In the *New Yorker* Pauline Kael had written: 'Los Angeles has become what it is because of the bright heat, which turns people into narcissists and sensuous provocateurs.' That alchemic attraction, if attraction it ever was, had ceased to work its magic on Christie. *Shampoo* signalled goodbye to a transient delight, a vacation for 'neurotic, inferior' Christie. Britain, she'd always said, could swallow her up without as much as a gulp: in London she was just

With Beatty *in flagrante delicto* in *Shampoo*

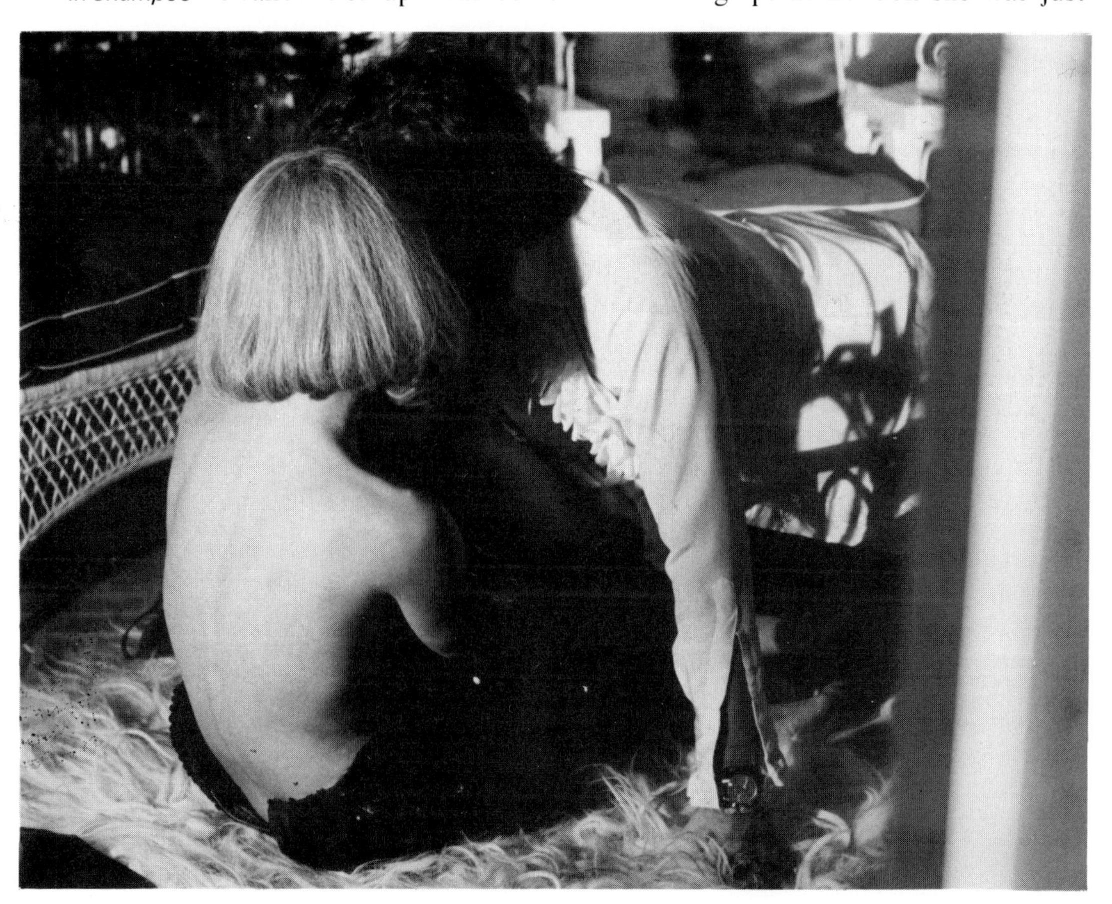

another face. Like Kipling said, there was no fame at home. At home she was no one.

Shortly after *Shampoo* was finished she flew to Britain, house-hunted and quickly found a property – a large grey farmhouse at Cefn-y-Coed, near Montgomery in Wales, called quixotically The White House, surrounded by acres of pasture land she immediately decided to sell off. Into this new haven she installed two San Francisco friends, artists Leslie and Jonathan Heale, not just as convenient factotums but in her old tradition, as 'mates' to pave a peaceful way. Then, because America still had some bind on her – she was contracted to one more feature film and was still intimately involved with some unnamed businessman – she flew back. But her days there were numbered.

Christie made two more films over a three year period in America, neither of them especially memorable in her sparkling *oeuvre*. *Demon Seed* (1977), for director Donald Cammell – who had made *Performance* with Nic Roeg, then fell out of favour with Hollywood – was controversial but far lesser in every respect than Beatty's *Heaven Can Wait*. Based on a trendy sci-fi novel by Dean Koontz about a scientist (Fritz Weaver) whose Frankenstein, a super computer called Proteus IV, goes haywire and decides to procreate with the creator's wife (Christie), *Demon Seed* gained attention thanks to extensive press coverage of a non-existent 'rape' scene, in which Proteus violates Christie, whom he holds captive in her own super-automated home. The muddled moral of the tale had something to do with machine-age alienation – best defined by the breakdown in understanding between scientist and wife, each obsessively involved with their own interests – but the film was shot, erroneously, for suspense and horror.

Ultimately, judged against its genre, *Demon Seed* collapsed. John Pym in the *Monthly Film Bulletin* found himself, like so many, irritated by the illogicality of Christie's methods of escape when held captive, and the special effects – which no such movie is decently presentable without – might have been seen on the wall of any discotheque ten years before. *The Guardian* found *Demon Seed* 'tedious' and Alan Brien in the *Sunday Times* berated 'a shallow exercise in bastard SF which does not even conform to its own rules'. Richard Schikel in *Time* signposted the one route towards some appreciation: the arcane cub philosophy that motivates this all-knowing genius computer. It seemed, guessed Schikel, to be fixated on two sources: de Sade (for its unremitting brutality) and Kahlil Gibran (from whom it borrowed its sententious prose style). No one much liked the predictable end where, having 'borrowed' the Christie character's womb, the computer begets a child identical to the one she recently lost to leukaemia. And no paying customers, attracted by the promise of some vicarious, if robotic, sensual pleasure with Darling Christie, liked being ripped off by the timid and polite 'rape' scene (in fact, the *accouchement* was the gratuitous shock effect scene, maximizing screams and writhings).

Cornered and questioned by *Newsweek* about her choice of involvement in this 'dreadful ménage à 3-in-1' (Proteus was assisted by an aide-de-camp, a mechanized wheelchair called Joshua the Blue Arm), Christie would only reply, tartly, that she liked action and she hadn't lately had the opportunity to 'fall into pits or be showered with sparks'. In truth, Christie's stop-start film activities over five years – coupled with the still-fresh memory of one or two big box-office flops – had reduced the range of properties on offer to her. The tendency, after *Shampoo* – as happens to so many stars – was to attract exploitive pseudo versions of what had scored before, rubbish scripts. According to friends, she probably wanted to undertake more work than she actually did, but her own high standards restricted her.

It took old mate Beatty – temporarily between lovers – to revive her once again with a jolly if not inspired script that had its artistic merits and looked sure to earn some money. *Heaven Can Wait,* a remake of the 1941 *Here Comes Mr Jordan* (not to be confused with Lubitsch's *Heaven Can Wait* which took the stage play's title but devised a new comedy) was given to Christie in the early summer of '77 at a time when, by all accounts, she was winding down her American life. Significantly she had also agreed to star in British director Michael Apted's *Agatha,* to be shot in England later in the year on a relatively small budget. *Agatha* would be her first truly British picture since *The Go-Between.*

Heaven Can Wait was a frothy, ill-fitting farewell to America, appropriate only in that it exercised yet again aspects of the real-life Christie – this time her new-found extracurricular interest in societal and ecological problems – though only on a superficial level. The story told of a second-rate U.S. football quarterback, Joe Pendleton (Beatty), who is involved in a serious traffic accident on the eve of the big Superbowl game. Taken for dead by the impatient archangel Mr Jordan (James Mason in fine form), Joe is taken to a heavenly way station from where, pleading his case, he is allowed to return to earth in a 'borrowed' body – that of millionaire businessman Farnsworth, currently in the process of being killed by his wife and male secretary (Dianne Cannon and Charles Grodin). Rich and influential as Farnsworth, new dimensions open for Joe – but he dedicatedly continues to prepare for the important ball game and successfully enlists the belief and support of his old coach Corkle (Jack Warden). As Farnsworth, he is constantly harassed by Betty Logan (Christie) who has come from England to contest the new refinery Farnsworth is building near her village – sequences which allow Christie to wax

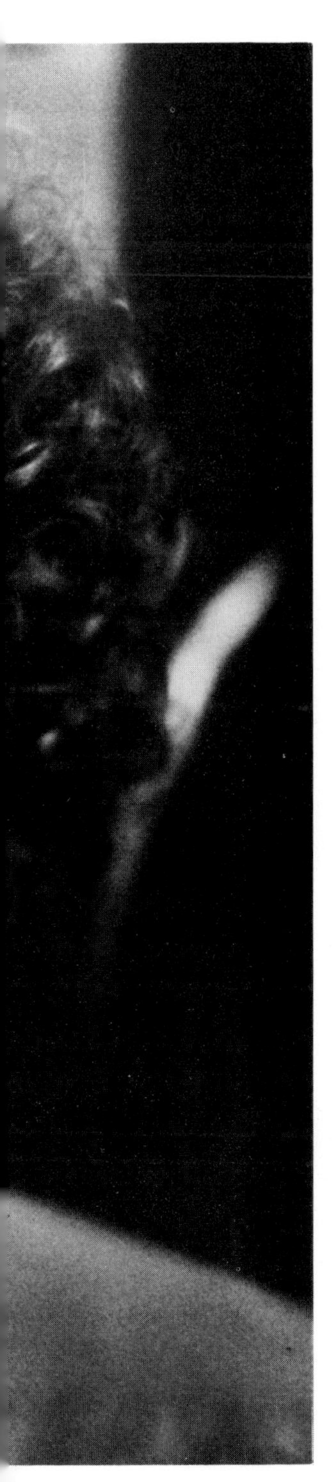

eloquently about conservation and the rights of man. Joe/Farnsworth eventually helps Betty – and *buys* the Rams football team so that he can play at the big match. Finally, when Farnsworth is at last successfully murdered by the conspirators, Mr Jordan gives Joe another 'borrowed' body: hereafter he will be stricken quarterback Tom Jarrett and will live on in that guise, with no memory of past lives. Joe/Jarrett meets Betty after the big game and, to their surprise, they are oddly instantly attracted to each other. . .

Heaven Can Wait made its way at the box-office but earned the kind of notices that decisively swung Beatty away from comedy towards loftier projects like *Reds* (1981). Neither Beatty nor Christie came over particularly strong in their respective parts and, most critics agreed, directors Buck Henry (who also starred) and Beatty plodded heavily through territory formerly pranced over by more-attuned forties' directors like Capra and Howard Hawks. Richard Combs, the critic, thought Julie Christie 'just shrill and woebegone in this fluffy fairy-tale context' and others sighed morosely, yearning for the days of strength and substance.

Long before the movie went on circuit release early in '78 Christie had, in the words of a friend, 'leapt feet first into the public pool' with the banners of her new pet interests. While still filming, she flew back to Britain to negotiate *Agatha,* met with some radical 'nuclear age' reformers in Wales and lent her name to a campaign that demanded reevaluation of the risks of nuclear waste. Christopher Hitchins of the *Daily Express* met her, half-expecting that 'stench of publicity-seeking . . . (which is) often to the detriment of the cause'. Instead he discovered her deeply and honestly involved, 'nervous and intense as she sat at a table piled high with books, cuttings and scientific magazines . . . She has really done her home work.' The only interviews Christie allowed during her short stay concerned this new campaign. The moment, she judged, was crucial, the issues too urgent. Just then Britain was deciding whether or not to become the country where the world's nuclear waste was processed to make plutonium, often called the most deadly substance in existence – 'so lethal it does not even occur in nature'.

A Royal Commission set up to examine the subject, and the new reactor at Windscale, Cumberland, now known as Sellafield, which would do the dirty work, had recommended 'extreme caution', in particular stressing the dangers of plutonium falling into the wrong hands. As a result, a public enquiry had been ordered but the official pro line was 'lavishly represented by expensive lawyers and experts – all appearing at the taxpayers' expense'. The main aim of the Christie-led campaign was that those who object to 'turning Britain into a nuclear society' should *also* be given public money to make their case.

What most appalled her, Christie said, was the lack of media exposure of true developments. 'Already the business of disposing of the live waste is creating a terrifying problem,' she asserted. 'Crates of waste deposited in the sea have been leaking. There have been accidents unforseen by the scientists in charge. Nonetheless, the government wishes to expand the monster it has created.'

Questioned about the origin of her concern, Christie ascribed it to her time in America. A period of relative film inactivity had allowed her to study up. She liked the way the Americans dragged dirty linen into the open, the fact that President Carter had called a halt to the plutonium reactor system and its further development. But in Britain, surreptitiously, the era of Big Brother was sweeping in, uncontested. Already the Atomic Energy Force was an armed wing of the police. Whatever happened to Tony Benn's promised Great Debate on the nuclear issues? Who asked the man in the street what *he* wanted? And how many ordinary folk bothered to challenge inscrutable 'official lines'? Returning after so long an absence Christie detected a tiredness of spirit in Britain that roused her. 'It just seems that there is so much more apathy here. People just leave things to the government.'

'A lot of the new high profile quasi-political image had to do with Beatty,' a colleague contends. 'She may have inspired him to certain socialist values or interests, but he himself was very active politically – and it rubbed onto her, started her going.' Indeed, there were those who claimed the sudden burst of involvement with the anti-nuclear league presaged a British political career – though Christie seemed temperamentally unsuited for that. Beatty's burgeoning interests probably did, however, inspire her somewhat. In the middle of his relationship with Christie he had, for almost two years, consistently promoted George McGovern's campaign for the 1972 Presidential Election.

McGovern said of him: 'He has a political maturity astounding to someone so inexperienced – the instincts of a man who has spent a lifetime in politics.' In fact, Beatty's political associations reach back to friendship with Bobby Kennedy, whom he briefly worked for. By '72 Beatty was pledged to the Democratic party, finding it 'intolerable to live in a country where Richard Nixon was President . . . It wasn't possible to be very interested in movies at that period.' Such social conscience was, of course, amply, independently, fed by Christie from the start. And then, apparently, the wheel turned full circle.

Agatha, the movie set to reinstate Christie as International British Star *in situ,* staggered dangerously from the start. Set up by whizz-kid ace David Puttnam with the coup of Dustin Hoffman's participation on a meagre £1.5 million budget, the film, which fictionally speculated on writer Agatha Christie's mysterious brief disappearance in 1926, first met flak from Agatha Christie's family, who opposed the project.

Previous page: In *Heaven Can Wait,* 1977

Then the employment of Italian cameraman Vittorio Storaro with his own full crew, arriving straight from the success of Coppola's *Apocalypse Now,* gave rise to objections – until Puttnam made it clear that five top British cinematographers approached had proved unavailable. Though Storaro, one of the highest-paid cameramen in Europe, was entitled to work in Britain (under Treaty of Rome regulations, as a citizen of a Common Market country), the UK technicians' union, the ACTT, only consented to allow him 'because it's going to be a non-British quota picture and therefore not entitled to Eady Levy'. Alan Sapper, ACTT general secretary, emphasized that he had advised the Department of Trade of the situation, which elicited the sour response from producer Gavrick Losey: 'The film's eligibility for Eady at the end of the day is a matter between the auditors and the Board of Trade – and not for the trade union movement to decide.'

In this sparky atmosphere, with Hoffman chomping at the bit and Apted properly scripted and ready to roll, the bad news came from L.A.: Christie, polishing off her work on *Heaven Can Wait,* had broken her wrist in an off-the-set roller skating accident. Beatty was forced to hold up his film's completion for six weeks, at huge cost – and a grim shadow fell over *Agatha.* Apted rushed to recast and auditioned a host of old-timers and new faces. Young New Zealander Helen Morse, with just a smattering of principal roles in TV, was provisionally engaged, to take over should Christie be unready when filming started the last week in October.

On October 28th *Screen International* announced the imminent start of *Agatha* – 'with Vanessa Redgrave (in the lead), but possibly without Julie Christie'. Producer Losey was still saying he'd be glad to have her, even at that late date, but reports from the States indicated Beatty's movie was still going. In the end, Losey and Apted were forced to go with Morse playing the bright young girl who befriends Redgrave as the runaway Agatha Christie, and while the film took no money in America it was sufficiently slick to persuade the notoriously fussy Universal to back Apted, with no notable track record, as director on their major feature *Coal Miner's Daughter* (1980), a box-office smash.

With or without *Agatha,* it was goodbye to Hollywood for Christie: not a quick decision, but the culmination of months of self-questioning, years of an unease too rarely admitted. 'Suddenly one day I was forced to make a decision, America or Britain. I had some very dear friends there and I was in love with an American. No, it wasn't Warren Beatty – by then he'd become one of my very dear friends. There were months of unhappiness when I couldn't make up my mind whether to leave or not. Choices are hard. It is easier to let things roll on. But at last I packed my bags and came home. I'd been away so long I saw England quite freshly.'

As with the stop-over the year before, Christie's fresh view of Britain stirred her new interests – those of social reformer – right across the boards. Every new experience in Britain was rousing or simply disturbing. 'People looked very poorly dressed and the pavements looked grubby.' The midnight mates in Earl's Court, brewing rebellion over cold coffee and metholated cigarettes, were utterly forgotten. 'I'd got use to those pavements in L.A. with not a spot on them – that's because no one walks on them! – and people wearing clothes that looked as though they'd been to the dry cleaners every day.' But the goods and bads of both worlds were sharply identifiable now. The scales tilted in favour of Britain for so many reasons: though in certain areas people needed to be informed, possibly led, 'it was good to be back in a place where folk were still conscious of the source of things; I'm sure some children in America think meat is born in plastic bags.'

Selwood Terrace had been sold in the transfer to Hollywood and now a new rented home was acquired, a flat in a large rambling house in Notting Hill Gate, crammed with mementoes of America, few of

Hollywood. For a time in London she was truly alone, freer and lonelier perhaps than she had ever been. The kind of American and British scripts offers still trickling in didn't interest her at all. She concentrated on phoning a few old friends, keeping abreast with the anti-nuclear movement checking decoration progress at the farm in Wales, finding her feet in London again. For six months nothing happened on the film front. Over New Year '78 she met and fell for rock musician-producer Brian Eno, late of Roxy Music. He was seven years her junior and the disparity, inevitably, delighted the press, a fair section of which had little time for crusading out-of-work actresses. For them she was 'faded sixties star', 'once the film world's cipher for the sixties'. The *Daily Express* had her, in February, at a rock person's party, alone. 'She looked very much the wallflower without him [Eno],' said a friend. 'She was looking rather dowdy in ankle-socks and sandals – rather like Mrs Mopp.' The mouse-like attitude, the *Express* concluded, was brought about by Eno's departure to Germany, where he was producing a series of American groups.

The *Express* quoted an actress associate who had shared an overnight sleeper compartment in Rumania during the RSC tour many years before: 'Julie is a bit scatty and very highly strung . . . but a warm and friendly girl.'

There was something grotesquely epitaphic about all press coverage of the return. Worse: it was banal and patronizing, reminiscent of those terrible early days when cliché substituted for comment, as though nothing worthwhile was being attempted or accomplished.

Christie cannot have missed the tone. But whereas before, in the Beaconsfield pin-up days, it enraged her, now perhaps it was no less than she was due. Her last estimable work was five years before and still she was only thirty-six, in the prime of her life. As for her nuclear reform campaigning – that, till now, had been desultory, a snatch between other schedules.

As the relationship with Eno petered out, new resolve coarsed through her. The Heales had the Welsh farmhouse refurbished and ready and she began to enjoy the solace of isolation in the desolate marshes, following her mother's footsteps. Simultaneously she intensified her crusading, attending lectures in Wales, broadening her knowledge of the British nuclear involvement. And, away from the distractions of city life, she found at last a script that teased her inherent, too often modified artistry. This time it was her choice, fully hers. The script was called *Sophie and the Captain,* French-written, about a free-living marriage where the husband is slowly turned to transvestism by his wife's lesbian obsessions.

Some said it would be as shockingly trend-setting as *Last Tango in Paris*. Others predicted disaster.

THE QUIET SURVIVOR

Julie Christie is not, never has been, an aggressive feminist. Her espousal of causes in the late seventies and early eighties – the anti-plutonium issue was to be first of several – inevitably earned her some cynical derision. But her detractors were unkindest when they spoke of her as tough and hearty, a hard-necked man-hater who enjoyed verbal combat for the hell of it. On the contrary, in all her angry sorties, she deported herself with dignity and displayed great qualities of intelligence, dedication and loyalty.

The greatest movie disaster of her career, *Sophie and the Captain,* tested her mettle as never before and served well to reveal her true values. She had not, as many claimed, been attracted to the project solely because an offbeat, some said radical director was at the helm; neither had she latched onto the purely commercial aspects of a conveniently controversial production. When director Liliane De Kermadec sent her the script she agreed to do it simply because she liked it.

By her own account she was financially secure enough not to *have to* work again but De Kermadec's tack excited her. 'It was,' Christie later said, 'a formidable experience for me to find a talent such as hers.' The script, largely written by Charlotte Crozet and Bernard Noel, was one De Kermadec had been hawking around for years, trying to set up for production in France. Finally a co-financing deal cobbled up by producers Serge and Irene Silberman with a TV company, SFP, paved the way and casting began. De Kermadec's experience was limited, but her work had attracted serious attention in Europe. She had started with experimental shorts and graduated to a feature, *Aloise,* which earned actress Delphine Seyrig a special mention at the 1975 Cannes Festival.

In *Memoirs of a Survivor,* directed by David Gladwell, 1980

Sophie and the Captain was De Kermadec's all time pet project, something she was prepared to sell her soul to do. As it happened, in the contract she signed with the Silbermans she signed away everything but her soul. Irene Silberman took a certain part in revising the script, and stipulated co-authorship credit for her efforts – a concession De Kermadec was happy to make. At that point however, as the script was launched into production with Julie Christie as the main star, all pretence to happiness and plain sailing died. The film was budgeted at $2 million and involved almost two months' shooting. But after two weeks, having seen the rushes of De Kermadec's and Christie's work, the Silbermans decided to stop the film. A spokesman for them said: 'It was simply a question of taste. The Silbermans found that the fine script was just not in the rushes and decided to call it off.' They would rather lose $100,000, it was said, than $2 million and they had a responsibility to their partner investors.

De Kermadec and Christie were incensed. Both felt their work was well up to standard and the flames were fanned when Irene Silberman intimated her real reasons for calling the halt: De Kermadec was shooting something different from the script and that was unacceptable. De Kermadec immediately sought and received the support of the Society of French Film Directors. Their communique stated that a director should not be judged on rushes and should be allowed to complete the film, since he or she is, after all, the ultimate author. But the Silbermans responded by stating that producers also had some authorial status: in Irene Silberman's case she would actually have co-screenplay credit. SFP's contribution was too small to give them any say, so the film was effectively stillborn in July '78.

Variety cheerily reported developments: Serge Silberman had been in films for over thirty years and had made five pictures with Luis Bunuel; there were no financial woes on the English-language *Sophie*, it was merely a decision that the film was not worth completing – it wasn't good enough. In an offensively cavalier tag *Variety* added: 'So far, no femme lib has popped up to champion director De Kermadec's case. She is being treated as a director irrespective of sex.' On the other side of the coin, callous observers noted that 'the feminists closed ranks'.

Julie Christie did speak out boldly in defence of De Kermadec – and herself. But she was just one of many – distinguished film men and women – who countered the Silbermans' quick and cold approach. 'I consider that I've been badly treated,' Christie said. 'I have never before heard of such conditions being imposed on an actor. As with every actor, I work with the director of the film, and if there is any problem it is with the director I discuss and solve it. As it happens, I found Liliane's work was formidable and I know that she was happy with mine. It is scandalous that an actor, engaged by both producer and director, should be dismissed by the producer without consultation with the director.'

But the Silbermans' book was closed. Recovering from a motor car accident in America, Serge Silberman and his wife duly paid off the contracted players and crew. Ironically, maddening to Christie and De Kermadec, the total fees pay-out was high, bringing the estimated loss to $700,000, almost half the projected film budget. Christie's pay-off was 'a five-figure sum' – considerably less, no doubt, than she had been getting in the States but certainly the biggest here involved. Still, it wasn't compensation enough. The cancellation of the film reflected badly on her and worried her agents and close associates who might have felt, not unreasonably, that continued credibility depended on a good European film soon.

But Christie's concern was all for De Kermadec and *her* reputation. Throughout frustrated months of protest she repeatedly demanded De Kermadec's reinstatement and when that was obviously no longer practicable in October she specially flew to Paris for a one-day visit to attend a press conference in which the Film Directors' Association put the defence case to the world. Christie spoke more that day than she'd done in three years. Sitting alongside De Kermadec she defiantly insisted that the picture was good, that De Kermadec knew her stuff. 'It is important,' she insisted, 'that the cinema should not lose a talent like this.'

The battle by now centred on the rights of authorship of *Sophie and the Captain* and the possibly exploitive factors of the Silbermans' contract with the director. Jerome Kanapa, general secretary of the Directors' Association, outlined the complex producers/director contract and described it as 'an incredible document'. He said the association was contemplating legal action and might ask Pierre Viot, director of the National Cinema Centre, the French film governing board, to intervene. It was also planned that Jacques Ralite, chairman of the cinema industry committee at the French Parliament, would raise the affair in the National Assembly. To each and all of these suggestions Christie gave full support. Her friend, French director Bertrand Tavernier (who would shortly use her to voice-over French actress Thérèse Liotard in his *Deathwatch*), was drawn in in support of De Kermadec too. From the conference table he spoke stoutly about De Kermadec's talents and was applauded by luminaries like Alain Resnais and Agnes Varda. Tavernier had even tried to act as mediator: 'It was incredible that the film should be stopped the way it was. I saw Serge Silberman, who was fantastically cordial and said he agreed the film must be saved. Subsequently however, every effort ran into closed doors.'

The fight, like the film, fizzled. Christie's altruistic concern to see justice done and De Kermadec get her chance to shoot the project that she 'so badly wanted' went largely unnoticed in the popular press. In their eyes, quite simply, the old star failed. The contractual irregularities, financial question marks – perhaps most importantly, personality conflicts – drew hardly a mention. Christie failed, the consensus implied, because she was vain, too powerful, out of condition, anachronistic, indifferent – or just plain found out.

Of more interest to the dailies and showbiz mags was the new love in her life, Scottish left-wing news editor of *Time Out* magazine, thirty-three year-old Duncan Campbell. Their friendship had started in April, weeks before De Kermadec's film, and had developed with a confident ease unknown since before Beatty. In the summer they holidayed in Italy together and during the *Sophie* trials in Paris he regularly flew to her side. Campbell was the best of companions for her at this watershed time in her life – erudite, stable as a monument. But his left-wing leanings gave ammunition to Christie's detractors. Her financial contributions to alternative newspapers like *City Limits,* on which he later worked, didn't help either. 'I think she suffered two burdens,' says an old colleague, 'an absolute revulsion to self-promotion and her own uptightness which made it hard for her to face public questioners and put her points over. But she had all these issues she felt strongly about, comments she *wanted* to make.'

The restricting anguished shyness was still evident, for sure. At *Time Out*'s tenth birthday party, held at London's Lyceum ballroom, she was greatly embarrassed by the presence of story-hounding journalist guests. Confronted by the *Evening Standard* man and asked to account for her presence she stammered: 'I don't know really. . .' Then turned to a friend and pleaded: 'Tell me what I should say.' In desperation she told the *Standard*'s man: 'I really can't think what I can tell you that would be of any interest.' When cameramen zoomed in she 'entered a condition approaching apoplexy and fled.' Campbell was in the background to comfort her but once again all queries about possible long-term arrangements were parried and dashed.

'The idea that marriage means security is a myth,' Christie said a short time later. 'No one can attain real security.' She was, she said, not in any way religious and did not need the state to bless her chosen lifestyle. She told *Woman's Own* she would remain single and though her 'pal' – as nebulous and safe a euphemism as the colloquial 'mate' – lived in London she would abide in Wales hereafter, in the grey White House, surrounded by her happy mengerie. Campbell was, nonetheless, essential to her: 'I'm terribly dependent on him, so we travel backwards and forwards to see each other.'

The tranquillity of Wales and the unstrained constancy of the relationship with Campbell soothed Christie as no other arrangement had. Nuclear disarmament, animal rights and commitment to the environment became her staple conversation and study subjects. She became dedicatedly a fitness freak, lover of long walks and hard exercise. But, as always, it seemed, there were paradoxes and contradictions. 'Style of life matters to me very much,' she said. 'There are so many advantages to be taken from the natural way of life . . . it seems so *automatic.*' She was proud to say she didn't drive a car and forcefully argued with anyone who would listen – even the gutter press – about conservation. 'And yet,' says a BBC director, 'she had no compunction about polluting the atmosphere in others' cars.' He goes on: 'Whenever she took a train to Wales, since the station was about thirty miles from her farmhouse she'd cheerfully order up a taxi . . . which *seemed* ironical because, as most people read it, she was all out against pollutants of any sort and cars were a no-no.' Similarly, the same man recalls, Christie banned the use of conventional toilet paper in the farmhouse and insisted that old newspaper be used – 'because paper came from trees and toilet paper was an unnecessary luxury'. The idea was admirable but in practice there were problems. 'Week after week a friend of mine, a local oddjob man, was summoned to unblock the drains. It was costing her a paper fortune to avoid the use of tissues. It seemed crazy.'

At Julie Christie's Welsh farmhouse

Though she idled a lot in Wales, between bouts of leaflet-writing her commitment to films continued. In March '79 she was delighted to have the opportunity to join the jury at the Berlin Film Festival though again she used the opportunity of a solid soap-box to push, this time, for societal reform. In a brazen, risky statement she agreed with the walk-out protest the Russians and other Communist delegations had fired against Universal's *The Deer Hunter*. She argued that the movie depicted the Vietcong as subhuman and sadistic, cold-heartedly ignoring the valour that helped them effectively resist both French and American onslaughts. She contended it was 'not proper for the director (Michael Cimino) to argue "dramatic efficacy" as an excuse for his approach' and, though the Festival organizers stood by the propriety of showing the film, she totally condemned it. Unforgivably various papers in Britain, *Evening Standard* to the fore, sardonically reduced her statement to terms of professional jealousy, bumptiously observing 'the real truth': '*The Deer Hunter*, of course, is in direct competition for a bunch of Oscars with the comedy *Heaven Can Wait*. . .' Which made about as much sense as the declared losers heckling from the aisles as Oscar changed hands.

The month of March 1979, indeed the rest of the year, was tainted by an accident that horrifically reflected the early scene in *Don't Look*

Having tea with a neighbour in Wales

Now where Christie's screen child is drowned in a garden pool. Driving to Cefn-y-Coed with Duncan Campbell, Christie arrived to find her friend Leslie Heale who had been digging in the garden frantically searching for her young son Harry. Harry was just twenty-two months old, and had wandered off while his mother's attention was diverted. Minutes later Leslie noticed 'what looked like a grey rug' floating in the middle of the two-feet deep garden pond the family used to breed rare geese. Then the shock of realization dawned. 'I could see the figure under the water,' Leslie told the inquest in April. 'I waded in and pulled him out and ran to the house. His face was blue.' On the settee in the living-room Christie and Leslie tried to revive the boy. Two doctors were called and an ambulance, but by the time it arrived the boy was dead. Christie, like the Heales, was 'devastated' and refused to talk to anyone, least of all the flocks of press who arrived.

The rest of the year, like the months after the French film debacle, passed without any coordinated effort to resume movie-making. John Travolta, initially assigned to Paul Schrader's *American Gigolo* (Richard Gere eventually took the role), specifically asked for Christie as co-lead, but she turned him down flatly. Though Europe had so far been unkind to her, having made her decision about America she would not recant. Neither would she be deterred from that still-cherished ambition to 'simply be a good actress'. Her message to prospective producers was straightforward: 'I've always been choosy about my films and I've turned down scripts I didn't approve of sometimes, even with directors I wanted to work with. It's so difficult to be sure that a film will have a positive effect on people – but you can easily see which will be negative. There are streaks of militarism, sexism or sadism running through film after film now – you can't avoid it entirely or you would never work again. The trouble with working in Britain, and I will do, because I love it so much, is that the film industry here has been more or less abandoned. There's so much talent here, apart from all those who've been forced to leave for America. It's just too bad it's not appreciated and helped along.'

True to her promise, the first script that came along without shades of militarism or sexism she quickly latched on to. She had waited eighteen months for David Gladwell's *Memoirs of a Survivor* and was sufficiently inspired by the work to rush on to no less than three further major films within the next eighteen months.

The end of what the press called her 'period of seclusion' marked a time of sudden participation in very vigorous crusading for causes. Before *Memoirs* moved into production in the winter of 1980 she was 'out of hiding', frequenting meetings of Pandora, the anti-nuclear campaign group, attending town hall meetings, gathering signatures, even lobbying her old enemy the press. 'Nuclear bombs are not made by countries or governments or one individual,' she said. 'It's the huge multi-national corporations that are in the business of arms production! They are internationalists and have no allegiance to anything except profit. They can't be expected to care that their activities are poisoning our world, our bodies and our minds.' Explaining the nature of her interest she spoke of 'natural curiosity about such things' which led to the 'shattering' discovery for her about the dangers of nuclear waste. It was a hideous vicious circle, she claimed. Nuclear power meant nuclear waste, and nuclear waste provides the raw material for plutonium, the essential atom bomb ingredient. 'So the production of nuclear waste is a necessity to keep alive the fastest-growing industry in the world: the nuclear arms business. Was it any wonder I wanted to join with others who had reached similar conclusions, to do battle?'

A further renewed concern was the exploitation of animals in controlled experiments. Approached by American documentary-maker Victor Schonfield, she readily agreed to narrate his film about the abuses of laboratory work for free. 'Julie saw parts of the film and said I'd come to the right person,' Schonfield announced. 'She said she wanted to do it to help minimize the suffering of animals.' His documentary, *The Animals Film*, a heart-sickening study of how medical researchers and big firms use caged live animals to test drugs and domestic products, was screened by Independent Television in Britain in 1982. Its horrific depiction of rodents with electrodes buried in their heads and rabbits enduring eye-drop tests with toxic liquids caused shocked protest from viewers and mobilized sympathetic public feeling.

At the press talk to launch the film in London Christie appeared, Patty Hearst-like, in black beret and battle-dress trousers, flanked by hooded members of the Animal Liberation Front. She revealed that she wrote regular aggressive letters to manufacturers of soap powders and bleach, demanding to know what tests they ran on animals, and urged others to do the same. 'I try not to use any of the cosmetics or shampoos that have been tested on animals,' she stated, but agreed it was difficult to sort out the worthy ones. She condemned participants in laboratory arrangements and spoke of the 'enormous sacrifice' made by defenceless animals 'in order that we should have certain comforts and luxuries; capitalism invents things that have to be made.'

At the same time she was attending CND rallies in London and lending her voice to the Vegetarian Society. For the *Daily Mirror* she was becoming 'even more boringly committed than Jane Fonda'. She had, she agreed, temporarily been a recluse – 'but only from the film world, not the real world' – and, no matter what the papers said, was enjoying her right of free speech. Denied their pin-ups and tinsel-town gossip, the lesser journals bitched remorselessly: 'The real difference

between Julie and Fonda is that Fonda gets deluged with work offers regardless of her politics.' The *Mirror* did concede, however, her employment on the low budget ($1.9 million) *Memoirs of a Survivor:* 'She will forgo star-style fees and settle for actor's wages. Any extra she makes is likely to find its way back into CND.'

Such palpable taunting insult was smothered by the joy surrounding the return to films with *Memoirs*. She had, she said, decided to do the picture because of David Gladwell, a daring young director whose BFI Production Board film *Requiem for a Village,* all about the contrast in lifestyles of an old Suffolk village and today's concrete jungle, she had seen and admired. With echoes of the continued loyalty to De Kermadec as much as to Beatty she stated: 'I am invariably more interested in choosing a director, rather than role or subject.'

Memoirs, scripted by Gladwell and ex-BBC editor Kerry Crabbe from Doris Lessing's novel, was an efficient, fast shoot (necessitated by financial complications) in Norfolk and around various London derelict sites. Christie was pleased with the emotional intensity such time schedules evoked. 'Preproduction *and* filming took nine weeks,' she said appreciatively. 'In America films can take as long as three years to make.' A case in point, of course, was the marathon *Shampoo,* spanning six years from concept to screening. She laughed off allegations that the movie was a personal statement, a wry comment on impending nuclear destruction. Incontrovertibly the film said something about a future society's breakdown but the comments were Lessing's and Gladwell's and Christie's role, in and out of character, was fairly passive.

Reflecting on her political involvement as she moved to Paris to bury the ignominy of the past with a fresh French production, *Les Quarantiemes Rugissants (The Roaring Forties),* she defended herself with an offhand 'I'm just following conscience'. Over Easter '81 she flew home for a few days but skipped relaxation at the White House for the chance to rally near the endlessly controversial Greenham Common air base, soon to be a site for American Cruise missiles. Hundreds of young rock fans, impatient for their rock bands, jeered her but she won them over with throat-rending eloquence, damning the government which put defence before jobs. There was nothing self-serving about what she was doing, clearly, but she was still obliged to profess her commitment. 'I came,' she said 'because only by swinging public opinion are we going to make the government listen.' The fact that only 3,000 people, one quarter of the crowd expected, showed up, the fact that some resented her celebrity and others didn't even know who she was, did not dampen her enthusiasm. She had made her point.

Asked about her feminist leanings she was equally, humbly forthright: there was no bitterness. 'Feminism means that you

Previous page: With Leonie Mellinger in *Memoirs of a Survivor*

understand how very low the status of women is today. You only have to look at advertisements to see how the sex object mystique continues.' As a one-time victim of the mystique-manufacturing process, she more than most was qualified to catalogue its pitfalls from both sides. She thought it desirable that people be conditioned *not* to respond to a pretty face. 'There's much more joy in life if you can think, "OK, that's not a pretty face. . ." and not be comparing it with some stereotype. It's the same with men. If you go beyond pretty faces you have such a wide range to experience.'

Julie Christie entered the eighties, her fourth decade, in a stable state of mind formerly foreign to her: near serenity. The softening, most judge, was primarily the gift of Wales, of functioning free, without mentors and moguls and men with fat contracts.

'One of the sharpest things I remember about childhood in Sussex was an overwhelming response to nature. The incredible wonder, the order of it all, the seasons with something changing every second. The pattern of natural life is so stunning. . .'

For three years she had wallowed in it, absorbing its delights and its disasters. Out in the world again, doing what she wanted to do since childhood – acting, expressing herself honestly – she was armoured and equipped as never before. No one owned her. She owed nothing to no one. From now on she would only answer the dictates of conscience and responsibility. In so doing she would begin to create her richest, subtlest screen characters.

RETURNS

Director Michael Hayes, the man who first placed Christie before the raking Cyclops' eye of the camera lens in *A for Andromeda,* recalls driving down the M6 several years ago, in company of a nineteen-year-old female friend: 'It was the time of the big re-release of *Gone With the Wind* and we passed some hoarding which reminded me and I told my companion it was a fine movie and I'd take her to see it. I said, "The last time I saw that movie I brought Julie Christie." And she said "Julie *who?*" It was funny, she didn't honestly know who I was talking about although she was a very bright girl clued into what's what. But then one must remember that Julie's *fame* was entrenched so deeply in a specific period, the sixties, when she did all that breathless work. In the seventies many people had forgotten just how great she was. . .'

The eighties, in contrast, gave every indication of renaissance. Before her work on *Memoirs* was unveiled an assortment of reputable film-makers were seeking her services with good scripts. The Brent-Walker group were chasing her to co-star with Albert Finney and Martin Sheen in the $6 million *Loophole,* and Michael Klinger had announced his hot hopes of signing her for *Bite,* a Caribbean-set caper movie. Though all indications were that she would do *Loophole,* which only entailed a fortnight's work, she passed it up for the chance to return to France for Christian de Chalonge's film about a round-the-world sailor not unlike the tragic Donald Crowhurst.

Once again, script values decided the issue. *Loophole* was undeniably box-office, but Christie wanted another type of vehicle to recast her own image. Word of her new intentions spread fast and at last she attracted the kind of offers she'd long dreamt of. In the summer of '81 she was offered *The Gold Diggers,* a feature debut for experimental director Sally Potter, described as a spoof adventure yarn with marked feminist undertones. *The Gold Diggers* would be

In the television production of *Separate Tables*

crewed mainly by women and was one of three features announced for British Film Institute backing during '81–'82. Though some co-financing was to be sought from West German regional television station WDR in Cologne, *The Gold Diggers'* estimated budget was around the BFI average of $235,000. In such circumstances, *Variety* recorded, Christie would receive the same minimal rate as all other actors – a fee probably in four figures, quite a come-down from her reported plateau of $400,000 during the late sixties.

Christie was more concerned about notices than cash. She had just finished *Les Quarantiemes Rugissants* in Paris when *Memoirs* went on release to mixed, not always perceptive notices. Confusion arose from the difficulty of classifying the film, a visionary work that defied conventional narrative technique and, in book and faithful film adaptation, rewarded careful study of metaphor and imagery.

Christie played 'D', chronicler of a society in chaos, who looks down on the marauding gangs and rubbish-strewn streets from the fortress prison of her flat. Buffeted by inner dreams and longings, D finds an alternative world by stepping through the wall of her flat, like Alice through the Looking-Glass. Here it is Victorian England, the bosom of an unsettled family, harbingers, perhaps, of the decay to come. She flits between the two sides of her double life, always observing, never participating, and watches as her protege, Emily (Leonie Mellinger), becomes involved with vagrants' leader Gerald (Christopher Guard) and their efforts to control the violent scavengers fail. In a final scene that provides a message-of-hope, D has a moment of surreal self-realization as she sees herself examining a giant egg, symbol of some undiscovered future, as fragile and contained (and well structured) as the visited past. Emboldened, she goes through the wall to meet the present for the last time.

Those critics who deemed *Memoirs* a failure brought their wrath down on Gladwell whose fidelity to Lessing's 1974 novel they saw as a cop-out. In turgid, truculent narcissistic prose many a reviewer hoisted himself with his own petard, fondly imagining improbable ways of serving the message better. *Films Illustrated* berated, totally unreasonably, an over-literate movie, full of words and rhetoric, and sought some inner-world invention without once looking into Julie Christie's eyes. *Photoplay* was fairest, conceding 'a strong performance from Christie' in 'one of the most mystifying films I can recall'. Their reviewer cheerfully admitted 'it would take a mind of greater genius than I to determine what [the movie is about]'.

Most discerning of all, Maria Aitken in the *Mail* saw Christie 'shining with serenity and more beautiful than ever after four years' absence from the screen'. Noting reaction as Christie's strong point, Aitken went on to applaude 'this evidence of the blossoming of the British film industry'. Others joined the ovation and Christie's personal notices were largely eulogistic.

The price to pay for rebuilding the Christie image via association with high-brow quality films was considerable. Apart from her own reduction in fees, Christie accepted that limited-market films meant limited showings. Though producers Michael Medwin and Penny Clark were hopeful of some box-office impact with Christie's and Lessing's names, the film did poor business in its British theatrical release and was swiftly transferred to domestic video by EMI, co-owner of the project.

Similar box-office slackness affected her next two major choices, the French film and, more ambitiously, Alan Bridges's *The Return of the Soldier. Les Quarantiemes Rugissants* began life as 'The Last Strange Voyage of Donald Crowhurst' a documented account by Ron Hall and Nicolas Tomblin of Crowhurst's 1968 round-the-world race attempt. He cheated his way to victory by dawdling in the Atlantic then doubling back, but committed suicide before facing the consequence of his action and possible discovery. French producer-actor Jacques Perrin had striven for years to get the production going and only succeeded by forging a multi-partnership deal with various independent television-film financiers in Germany, France and Sierra Leone.

Introduced to Christie by mutual French friends, Perrin recognized her value as a ticket to assured international release. He approached her frankly and won her approval. The script, however, was sadly lacking – 'a poorly detailed script', by *Variety*'s reckoning – and improved little as the production advanced. What was planned as a small budget film eventually grew to a monstrous 29,000,000-franc venture that took more than ten months to complete, shooting in France and off the coast of West Africa. ($4 million, the approximate equivalent, is about twice the budget of the average French film). Christie played Englishwoman Catherine, wife of the failed electronics expert who is persauded by an unscrupulous press agent (Michel Serrault) into tricking the world in a round-the-globe attempt. Producer Perrin himself played Dantec, the mariner. The thrust of the narrative stayed with Dantec as he battled the elements in his trimaran and soliloquized about his fears and misfortunes, but frequent flashbacks showed his tense relationship with Catherine and the unhappy events which led to the voyage.

First opening in Paris, *Les Quarantiemes Rugissants* did poor business and caused *Variety* to predict recutting and shortening of what they judged an overlong, dramatically insipid production. Script, direction and casting were universally panned and the prognosis, in terms of its chances on the international circuit, was bad. Christie alone – yet again – emerged with some honourable credibility, though *Variety* cursed the scenes she was forced to play as 'especially trite'. Her role, they agreed, 'allows her little opportunity to make an impression' – indeed, in total time she is no more than a half-hour on screen. A pity, because latent aspects of the frustrated wife, threatening to erupt powerfully in successive scenes, might easily have been riveting, if given greater scope.

Retitled as *Roaring Forties* – a nautical allusion – the film found no ready distributors in the international sphere and expired quietly in Europe, but Christie had little time for dismay. Without any vacation, in an unbroken run reminiscent of her heyday, she sped through *The Gold Diggers,* the French film, and *The Return of the Soldier.*

The last named looked like a good choice. Adapted by prestige TV writer Hugh Whitemore from a novella by Rebecca West, it was to co-star Christie's trusted old mate Alan Bates, the multi-talented Ann-Margaret and, best lure of all, Christie's current favourite actress Glenda Jackson. The film appealed to her, Christie reported, on several levels: 'Glenda was one of the main reasons I did it. She's just so good and I admire her. And I was asked to play this part unlike any I had done before. I play a rather cold, rather selfish upper-class woman who cares more for form than for substance. It's an unsympathetic role.'

Alan Bridges, a tightly controlled director adept at such purist British drawing-room drama as *The Hireling* (1973) and the *Brief Encounter* remake (1976), brought the production in smoothly on time and on budget with no disruptions or tears shed. On set Christie had learnt new lessons about herself, and welcomed the experience. She found: 'I can't do what Glenda Jackson or Alan Bates can do, which is to have a joke off the set one minute and the next minute play a big emotional scene. I need to work up a lot to suffer on screen. Acting is an incredible intimacy with people you don't know and you have to learn to deal with that.' Her high-energy application had cleared some cobwebs in her own mind about her acting urge and this, to her close friends, was a moment of prime importance – a rare instance of Christie resolving one of her inner mysteries. 'I'm not exactly dedicated,' she told interviewer Joan Goodman, 'but I really love it. I suppose one might say that I don't love acting enough to act just for the sake of acting, which a lot of actors do – and I quite understand it because it's like a drug, it's such a wonderful thing to do. But every time I do it I think, gosh, what a gas!' Her main motivation wasn't money, rather the urge to express herself, and give entertainment within the confines of her principles.

Christie's character Kitty in *The Return* was her most pathetic yet curiously unsavoury creation since Darling Diana herself. A haughty society queen with a tunnelled view of life and love, Kitty's complacency is rocked when her husband (Bates) returns from the front during the First World War shell-shocked and suffering amnesia, not knowing who she is and determined for a reunion with a working class lover from his past (Glenda Jackson). Kitty employs a psychiatrist (Ian Holm) to help unscramble her husband's feelings for the women in his new disoriented life (Ann-Margaret makes up the triangle, playing a too-caring cousin), but ultimately comes to realize that the man she knew is unreachable, as dead as the past he pines for.

Christie expressed herself satisfied with *The Return:* 'I'm quite pleased with the way it came out, although it doesn't always have the simplicity I imagined it would,' – but the critics, especially in Europe, raved. At the Cannes Festival (where *Memoirs* had been commended the year before and where Bridges took a coveted Golden Palm for *The Hireling*), *The Return* was entered in competition but took no awards. Instead there was praise, lavish garrulous praise. Back in London, Milton Shulman blessed 'the haunting, hypnotic quality of the film' and the performances all round. David Castell in *Photoplay* celebrated 'a fine romantic picture about second chances and the impossibility of raising the past from its grave', and gave special praise to Christie who 'works wonder with an underwritten role'. To set the seal of approval Derek Malcolm in the *Guardian* welcomed Christie's 'opportunity to extend her range' in 'a well-made, well-acted and beautifully set in-period' piece – 'yet another British film well worth the admiration bestowed upon it abroad'.

Like *Memoirs, The Return of the Soldier* drew bad box-office and quickly found a new market outlet on home video, a short cut to profit returns (or at least break-even) for its producers.

It was, maddeningly, a time when gold was transformed to dross-status – an ironic reversal of her earliest days in cheapie films. But Christie did not alter course or pause for reassessment. She didn't need to. Broad commercial success was only desirable as a lever to keep her in business. And even that requirement needed qualification: she had no desire to repeat the constricting popularity boom of the late sixties, or the Hollywood days. Such success was self-defeating, allowed no chance for talent to develop. Making the BFI's *The Gold Diggers* in the summer of '81 had been, like *The Return,* a refreshing growth experience. Contrary to bush rumour, she had not 'dashed to the summons of the feminist cause'. In fact, she had approached the experimental production warily, like the novice to such work she was.

'When it was first explained to me I didn't understand a word of it,' she confessed frankly. 'It was very intellectual and sort of structuralist . . . I decided to do it even though the idea scared me. But in fact it turned out to be a wonderful experience.' The feminist associations had been more a pleasant surprise than anything. 'I have often found working on regular films that there's no one who shares my point of view. When you start talking of women in what is a male-dominated profession and you literally get laughed down, that's a lonely situation. It was a joy *not to be* in that situation.' The response from the heart

was one of gracious gratitude, not fist-waving, cause-making euphoria. *The Gold Diggers*, like all of her film experiences since the return to Europe, educated and enriched her. In this way, for the very first time, the movie business was truly rewarding Christie's starry twenty-year input.

When, a year after *The Gold Diggers*, old pal John Schlesinger reemerged with a TV project he particularly wanted Christie for, he found the process of negotiation far smoother than might have been expected. Luring any major actor into television work is never easy but Schlesinger, ardently committed to a small screen version of Terence Rattigan's 1954 twin-play, *Separate Tables*, discovered a transformed gentle giant. 'She used to be as acquisitive as me,' he said, 'but she doesn't need the trappings of success any more – which I think is an admirable quality.' Welsh life, he observed, brought out other qualities which made her even more alluring as an actress. The brittle edge of nervousness was gone and when finally she settled into the fast studio shoot, Schlesinger widely announced that the experience was 'a joy', largely because Christie had perfected the art of not 'wasting time on the inessentials'. Much as she loved Schlesinger she had, as ever now, taken some time to decently assess the rightness of the project: 'At first I found it hard to relate to the morals and attitudes of the characters . . . but I decided to go ahead because I really wanted to work with John and Alan [Bates] again and once I started . . . it wasn't a conflict for me.' *Separate Tables*, networked in America and Britain during 1983, won unanimous good notices and excited a new wave of interest in Julie Christie, especially in America.

As Joan Goodman observed, the transformation from flash sixties Darling to socially-committed heroine of low-budget eighties Britain paralleled the progress of the country itself. A hazy sense of rebelliousness had been traded for a focused set of worthwhile causes. The fool's wealth of the sixties was forgotten and new fortunes were found in adversity.

After her first four crammed 'return' films – four in just twenty months – the serene Julie Christie was beginning a new-born existence. It seemed no coincidence that India, her birthplace, the forgotten tabernacle of her innocence, suddenly beckoned.

The ballroom scene in *The Gold Diggers*

CHILD OF INDIA

In India, and after, the soul is bared. Those interviewers who catch Julie Christie will now net the truth about her. Those seeking to understand what precipitated her change from timid recluse to cool cause fighter will hear that she was, has too often allowed herself to be unconfident, impulsive, scared. Those are personality traits that will probably always haunt her, but she has isolated them now, knows the danger areas.

'Until very recently I couldn't stand to look at myself on the screen. I was so embarrassed. I couldn't bear to see this person all big like that, I hated it. But that neurosis is all gone. I *made* myself get out of it. It's like I've had to make myself not be frightened of snakes when I went into the desert. I worked at making myself get out of the fear and I've got out of it. You can't live like that.'

Gossip distresses her – whether it plays upon her public activities or her intimate life – but 'a lot of that's to do with making yourself too important and holding yourself and how people see you in too much esteem. With a little bit more humour and a little bit more lightness the whole thing could be the joke it really is.' As for detailed analysis of the past, mistakes and learning episodes – that is, will always remain, a void. She admits to no memory of incidents or dates, cannot even recall the title of 'that film I did with Warren about somebody who turns into a football player'.

This vagueness isn't deliberate – 'It's something I would very much like to get taken care of, and *will* get taken care of. I can't go on like this. I think it's a form of amnesia. . .' She remembers no detail further back than her return to Britain, setting up home in Wales. The public conception of Warren and Hollywood she finds sadly wrong: 'I wasn't with Warren that long, no longer than I'd been out with others, so people's consciousness of me is very much of a small period of my life. . .' But she will not, cannot assist in extending that. 'Nothing exists that's very far back in the past.'

In the award-winning *Heat and Dust*, 1982

Instead she can talk of now – of her Indian pilgrimage with James Ivory's *Heat and Dust,* filmed through the spring of '82, of her hardened fight against nuclear arms, her solidarity with the Greenham Peace Women, the laden, promising screen future. In the past, she says, she was not at all a secure woman and she hid behind strong men; now the quiet good example of feminism has steeled her, funnelled her neuroses into a manageably acceptable single burden: perennial self-consciousness.

The process, she admits, is scary and insidious. 'You don't even know it's going on, it just becomes part of you, like you were in a wheelchair, or slightly crippled. But you learn to live with it.' It affects her worst when she's out in the street, casually shopping 'with something awful on – say my nightdress with a coat over it because I can't be bothered. All the time there's a subconscious voice going, "I wonder who's going to look at me, I wonder who's going to notice, I wonder who's going to think this or that. . ."' Still, she *does* go shopping in her nightdress, and does mercilessly watch herself on the Big Screen, evaluating and criticizing. She still has fear, but her fears are less.

After the Cannes success of *The Return of the Soldier* Christie noted the unspoken expectation that she would offer herself as 'media fodder' – confessing which brand of cornflake she eats, what stars do in private, telling an anecdote or two. Maybe it was assumed she would be light-headedly grateful for resumed cinematic success. This time she met the press head on, granting interviews with alacrity. But her well-prepared responses were as effective as a well-writ obituary, closing the book forever on the glittering star image. She had recently taken part in a documentary about The Bomb for Channel 4 British Independent Television and the journalists who came to clinch their 'star exclusives' were thwarted with anti-nuclear information delivered with infectious passion. There was, they discovered, no other Christie extant.

Angela Neustatter went to talk to her about *The Return* and came back with the fact file on opposition to American deployment of Cruise missiles in Britain and Christie's commitment to the Peace Women's campaign: she was, she told Neustatter, keen to take a break from films 'to be Joan Slugg again, participating in what is going on . . . We have to do everything possible to stop Cruise missiles. . .' She recounted stories of her friendships with the Peace Women, her marginal work in Wales. Once or twice she had been to Greenham Common, the 'front line' of the Peace movement; she wanted urgently to spend more time there. 'One of my most powerful memories is of leaving Greenham on a bus I hired with some neighbours. The women were standing waving and shouting thanks for our support and I thought, here we are abandoning them and still they are thanking us.

Next time I shall go back and try to offer more.'

Outspokenly honest, she admitted to many the agonized difficulties of pairing her undying interest in acting with peace campaigning. For her as much as any woman, involvement in the Peace movement was no simple step. 'It is not in women's culture to get up off their arses and act.' Filmmaking, meanwhile, was an equal obsession, something she had to pursue.

Julie Christie describes BBC researcher Anne, the character she plays in *Heat and Dust,* a woman attracted to the mysteries of India and her family's past: 'She is eager and enthusiastic to learn, but has a lot of Western conditioning that has closed off part of her mind. She is unfulfilled professionally and emotionally, but in India she ceases to be lonely. She does not do this by finding a person, but by finding a way of thinking that does not demand that you should have such and such a man and such and such a job.'

In India with Ivory the new Christie was at her happiest. Technicians among the crew found her strange and remote, but grew to like her. Ivory found her relaxed and inventive, a treasure trove of gentle creations. She could not quite fit in to the work at first because she was overwhelmed by India and told everyone she felt as though she had been here indefinitely. 'I love India so much,' she said. 'I have

With Charles McCaughhan in *Heat and Dust*

never had this reaction to a place before.' She recognized the ironies and coincidences of the circumstances but chose to play them down. All she would tell anyone was that she was glad to be there and that her childhood had been too short. She had never understood her roots, the turbulent essence of colonial India; but now she said: 'I need to know.'

Heat and Dust, bestowed on her by the brilliant Ivory-Merchant director-producer team, was another of Ivory's explorations of the reconciliation of two cultures, Indian and British, old and new. The ramifications resoundingly echoed aspects of Christie's own experience.

She plays Anne, drawn to modern-day Satipur by the magical memories of her great-aunt's diaries – chronicles of a forbidden love affair in the clouded past. In smoothly alternating sequences Anne's journey of investigation and discovery is balanced against the trials and longings of great-aunt Olivia (Greta Scacchi) among the declining British ruling classes, at the Civil Lines in Satipur in the 1920s. Two love alliances develop – Anne's unforced friendship with her Indian guide Inder Lal (Zakir Hussain) and, in the flashback, Olivia's scandalous fling with the local Nawab (Shashi Kapoor). Both become pregnant but prevailing social values dictate different solutions: Olivia aborts her child but Anne, in greater command of her womanhood and destiny, goes serenely to the local hospital where her child will be born. As the critic Philip Strick remarked: for Olivia, from an inflexible background, the encounter with a continent in flux and its dangerous men is as a victim; for Anne, in the more tolerant atmosphere of the eighties, it seems possible to be a participant. 'The story speaks,' he wrote, 'of a long sought and finally achieved union between country and tourist, with no need for further abortions.'

In India, blissfully anonymous, Christie could let her hair down unselfconsciously, like she'd never done in twenty years of 'star' exposure. She dressed rough, lived rougher, dallied with the locals and tried to revive the Hindi she learnt as a kid. Director James Ivory's production team offered her the best room in the best five-star hotel in sweltering, rubbish-strewn Hyderabad. She refused, insisted on a scruffier real-life abode round the corner. On a trip into the centre of Hyderabad in search of the appropriate footwear for her role, she insisted on trying on every pair of sandals in the shop. She rejected every style, then spotted the ones she wanted on a customer who entered. The wardrobe mistress accompanying her discovered that the desired sandals had been purchased in Bombay. Julie wasn't deterred. 'Send to Bombay,' she instructed wilfully.

Clare Colvin of the *Daily Express* visited the location and realized the significance of the moment: 'I saw the beginning of the Indian love affair where Julie . . . was standing in the courtyard of a crumbling old

house lent by a local Nawab for location shots. She was barefoot and wearing a cotton skirt and T-shirt. A young Indian girl, one of the Nawab's family, shyly presented her with a fountain pen. Julie was overwhelmed by the generosity. She had admired the pen the day before and now the girl insisted on giving it to her.' Julie wanted to repay the kindness. She surveyed her luggage, her wardrobe, the accoutrements of a flashy rich life but found nothing worthy. Cartier, Van Cleef and Arpels quite simply don't equate with the hand-carved trivia of tribal life. 'Everything they have is so much more beautiful,' Julie moaned, genuinely aggrieved. Tender moments in India brought Julie Christie to the brink of loving tears. 'There was nothing superficial or affected about it,' says a publicist. 'She was spiritually, utterly, at home.'

Heat and Dust's timeliness and effectiveness for Christie could not have been more perfect. When the film ended and the crew dispersed, Duncan Campbell joined her in Hyderabad and they lost themselves in the Himalayas for several weeks, drifting. She was not of course, in the literal sense, a tourist. She was a child of India, a product of its heat and dust, and because of that the reconciliation was vibrant and intense. The process, absolving and educative and inspiring all at once, was like a time loop, swirling her back to the mystery of her childhood. With her new maturity and receptivity she *participated* this time and took away more perhaps than her mother Rosemary ever did, certainly more than that blue-eyed, mystified seven-year-old child who left a failing family life to venture into an insecure future.

Against the intensity of Christie's spiritual experience in India judgements on *Heat and Dust* seem almost redundant. It was, critically, a huge success – 'a sumptuous, sensuous, ravishing film' for the *Sunday Express*. 'A great film?' the *Daily Telegraph* speculated hotly. 'Perhaps posterity will say so. Meanwhile don't be put off by that big word and the suggestion of significance – every single scene is a joy visually and verbally. Quite simply superb.'

Though it looked certain to make money and once again expand the crowd-appeal of the actress, she seemed fully uninterested. After her Himalayan adventures she celebrated her British homecoming with letters of support to CND, petition-signing, sprightly lobbying. In December she was at the Greater London Council's headquarters with left-wing leader Ken Livingstone and Dean of St Paul's, the Rt Rev. Alan Webster, beneath a high-flying red flag, collecting anti-Cruise signatures.

Weeks later she was on the 'shadow' board of Barclays Bank – a group of top anti-apartheid campaigners who for three years had examined the bank's investments in South Africa and produced their own 'alternative' annual reports – hitting out against the bank's 'direct backing of the evil apartheid system'. Immediately after, she was on

Previous page: Offset with James Ivory in Hyderabad on *Heat and Dust*

television, virulently attacking abuses in the media, slamming 'the powerful myth that we are all well served by the broadcasting authorities' and supporting the Campaign for Press and Broadcasting Freedom.

The hidey-hole of Wales which had always been the background, became foreground. She tramped back there boldly, ready for the comical contradictions of everyday life – the jammed toilets and rising damp and peaceful disarray ('we are not self-sufficient, we are totally insufficient'). This time she even brought a film photographer with her, a keen and ingenious lensman called Chris Cormack whom she'd met on *Heat and Dust.* Cormack was assigned the task of showing the new Julie to the world.

'I stayed with her for a bit and took lots of shots,' he says. 'Years before she'd been pictured in the conventional down-on-the-farm dungarees-and-muck way. But she didn't want that anymore. She wanted a new image. And that new image was *no image.* She wanted to be photographed as *herself,* no faking.' The borrowed flat in Bayswater, property of a friend, was visited less often. Smokescreens, pretence, illusions were down. She gave freer interviews and made it clear that, despite her socio-political interests she was, by a fraction, an actress first. She could never see herself running for political office.

'No! No! I can't talk to *anyone.* I've tried and it's just not there. I'm not a person who is very good at [real life] dialogue. I get terribly fazed if somebody says something I think is wrong . . .' Her twenty-year career had afforded her a crystal perspective and the suggestion was made that her new maturity might encourage her to produce, maybe direct her own movies – something perhaps in the style of the yet-unseen *The Gold Diggers.* She shakes her head at the prospect. 'I'm not an organizer. I'm really a footsoldier in a way, rather than a general. It's a kind of fear, I suppose.'

In 1965 David Lean said of her: 'She is an independent creature with strong views of her own. She doesn't want to be turned into something off the conveyor belt. She won't be, either.' Looking back through the clarity of the British film renaissance and the Indian magnifying glass, it seems the odds were stacked heavily against her. She was too beautiful, too malleable, too celebrated, too mixed-up, too much loved.

But she kept moving, faster than any conveyor belt, and she survived. No Svengali, real or imagined, could hold her now. The consequent question poses itself: where does the happy survivor go next? There's a tender moment towards the end of *Heat and Dust* when Anne is preparing to go off and have her baby. Her lover sees the misty, yearning complexity of her expression.

'Thinking again?' he asks fondly.

Julie Christie smiles. The thinking process goes on.

FILMOGRAPHY

CROOKS ANONYMOUS (Great Britain, 1962)
Director: Ken Annakin. *Producers:* Julian Wintle and Leslie Parkyn. *Associate Producer:* Jack Davies. *Screenplay:* Jack Davies and Henry Blyth. *Photography:* Ernest Steward. *Editor:* John Trumper. *Art Director:* Harry Pottle. *Music:* Muir Mathieson and Henry Martin, with Muir Mathieson as Musical Director.
Production Company: Independent Artists. *Distributed by:* Anglo Amalgamated. *Running time:* 87 minutes. In black & white. Cert: U.

Dandy Forsdyke: Leslie Phillips, *Widdowes:* Stanley Baxter, *Montague:* Wilfrid Hyde White, *Babette:* Julie Christie, *Sir Harvey Russellrod:* James Robertson Justice, *Ronnie:* Michael Medwin, *Prunella:* Pauline Jameson, *Grimsdale:* Robertson Hare, *Fletcher:* Charles Lloyd Pack, *Holding:* Bryan Coleman, *Woods:* Harry Fowler, *Wagstaffe:* Raymond Huntley, *Thomas:* John Bennett, *Grogan:* Arthur Mullard, *Jones:* Arthur Lovegrove, *Carol:* Joyce Blair, *Drunk:* Colin Gordon.

THE FAST LADY (Great Britain, 1962)
Director: Ken Annakin. *Producers:* Julian Wintle and Leslie Parkyn. *Screenplay:* Jack Davies and Henry Blyth. *Photography:* Reg Wyer. *2nd Unit Director:* Don Sharp. *2nd Unit Photography:* Michael Reed. *Editor:* Ralph Sheldon. *Art Director:* Harry Pottle. *Music:* Norrie Paramor.
Production Company: Independent Artists. *Distributed by:* Rank. *Running time:* 95 minutes. In Eastman Colour. Cert: A.

Charles Chingford: James Robertson Justice, *Murdoch Troon:* Stanley Baxter, *Freddy Fox:* Leslie Phillips, *Mrs Staggers:* Kathleen Harrison, *Claire Chingford:* Julie Christie, *Wentworth:* Eric Barker, *Bulmer:* Oliver Johnston, *Bodley:* Allan Cuthbertson, *Lady on zebra crossing:* Esma Cannon, *Shingler:* Dick Emery, *Dr Blake:* Deryck Guyler, *Policeman:* Victor Brooks, *Police motor cyclist:* Terence Alexander, *First Bandit:* Danny Green, *Second Bandit:* Michael Balfour
with guest appearances by Fred Emney, Frankie Howerd, Monsewer Eddie Gray, Raymond Baxter, Graham Hill, John Bolster and John Surtees.

BILLY LIAR! (Great Britain, 1963)
Director: John Schlesinger. *Producer:* Joseph Janni. *Associate Producer:* Jack Rix. *Screenplay:* Keith Waterhouse and Willis Hall. Based on the novel by Keith Waterhouse and the play (same title) by Waterhouse and Willis Hall. *Photography:* Denys Coop. *Editor:* Roger Cherrill. *Assistant Directors:* Frank Ernst and Jim

Brennan. *Art Director:* Ray Simm. *Music:* Richard Rodney Bennett.
Production Company: Vic Films in association with Waterhall. *Distributed by:* Warner-Pathe/Anglo Amalgamated. *Running time:* 98 minutes. In black & white Cinema Scope. Cert: A.

Billy Fisher: Tom Courtenay, *Liz:* Julie Christie, *Geoffrey Fisher:* Wilfred Pickles, *Alice Fisher:* Mona Washbourne, *Florence, grandmother:* Ethel Griffies, *Duxbury:* Finlay Currie, *Arthur Crabtree:* Rodney Bewes, *Barbara:* Helen Fraser, *Eric Stamp:* George Innes, *Shadrack:* Leonard Rossiter, *Rita:* Gwendolyn Watts, *Det. Insp. MacDonald:* Patrick Barr, *Disc Jockey:* Godfrey Winn, *Prison Governor:* Ernest Clark, *Danny Boone:* Leslie Randall, *Mrs Carbtree:* Anna Wing.

YOUNG CASSIDY (Great Britain, 1964)

Director: Jack Cardiff (some sequences directed by John Ford). *Producer:* Robert D. Graff and Robert Emmett Ginna. *Associate Producer:* Michael Killanin. *Screenplay:* John Whiting. Based on *Mirror in my House* by Sean O'Casey. *Photography:* Ted Scaife. *Editor:* Anne V. Coates. *Production Supervisor:* Teddy Joseph. *Assistant Director:* John Quested. *Art Director:* Michael Stringer. *Music:* Sean O'Riada, with music direction by Marcus Dods. *Costumes:* Margaret Furse.
Production Company: Sextant – A John Ford Film. *Distributed by:* MGM. *Running time:* 110 minutes. In Technicolor. Cert: A.

Johnny Cassidy: Rod Taylor, *Mrs Cassidy:* Flora Robson, *Nora:* Maggie Smith, *Daisy Battles:* Julie Christie, *Lady Gregory:* Edith Evans, *W.B. Yeats:* Michael Redgrave, *Archie:* Jack MacGowran, *Ella:* Sian Phillips, *Tom:* T.P. McKenna, *Sara:* Julie Ross, *Michael:* Robin Sumner, *Mick Mullen:* Phillip O'Flynn, *Bessie Ballynoy:* Pauline Delaney, *Undertaker's man:* Donal Donnelly, *Foreman:* Arthur O'Sullivan.
Note: In mid-production director John Ford withdrew from the film through illness.

DARLING (Great Britain, 1965)

Director: John Schlesinger. *Producer:* Joseph Janni. *Associate Producer:* Victor Lyndon. *Screenplay:* Frederic Raphael. *Photography:* Ken Higgins. *Editor:* James Clark. *Production Manager:* Ed Harper. *Set Decorator:* David Ffolkes. *Art Director:* Ray Simm. *Music:* John Dankworth.
Production Company: Vic/Appia. *Distributed by:* Warner-Pathe/Anglo Amalgamated. *Running time:* 127 minutes. In black & white. Cert: X.

Robert Gold: Dirk Bogarde, *Miles Brand:* Laurence Harvey, *Diana Scott:* Julie Christie, *Malcolm:* Roland Curram, *Sean Martin:* Alex Scott, *Alec Prosser-Jones:* Basil Henson, *Felicity Prosser-Jones:* Helen Lindsay, *William Prosser-Jones:* Tyler Butterworth, *Estelle Gold:* Pauline Yates, *Lord Grant:* Peter Bayliss, *Prince Cesare Della Romita:* Jose-Luis De Villalonga, *Raoul Maxim:* Jean Claudio.

DOCTOR ZHIVAGO (USA, 1965)

Director: David Lean. *Producer:* Carlo Ponti. *Executive Producer:* Arvid Griffen. *Screenplay:* Robert Bolt. Based on the novel by Boris Pasternak. *Photography:* Freddie Young. *Editor:* Norman Savage. *Production Managers:* Augustin Pastor and Douglas Twiddy. *2nd Unit Director:* Roy Rossotti. *2nd Unit Photography:* Manuel Berenguer. *Assistant Director:* Roy Stevens. *Production Designer:* John Box. *Art Director:* Terence Marsh. *Set Decorator:* Dario Simoni. *Special Effects:* Eddie Fowlie. *Music:* Maurice Jarre. *Costumes:* Phyllis Dalton.
Production Company: Carlo Ponti. *Distributed by:* MGM. *Running time:* 193 minutes

(plus 4-minute overture and two minutes intermission music). In Metrocolor Panavision 70mm. Cert: A.

Yuri Zhivago: Omar Sharif, *Lara:* Julie Christie, *Tonya:* Geraldine Chaplin, *Komarovsky:* Rod Steiger, *Yevgraf:* Alec Guinness, *Pasha/Strelnikov:* Tom Courtenay, *Alexander:* Ralph Richardson, *Anna:* Siobhan McKenna, *The girl:* Rita Tushingham, *Sasha:* Jeffrey Rockland, *Yuri at 8 years old:* Tarek Sharif, *The Bolshevik:* Bernard Kay, *Kostoyed:* Klaus Kinski, *Liberius:* Gérard Tichy, *Razin:* Noel Willman, *Medical professor:* Geoffrey Keen, *Amelia:* Adrienne Corri, *Petya:* Jack MacGowran, *Engineer at Dam:* Mark Eden, *Old soldier:* Erik Chitty, *Beef-faced Colonel:* Roger Maxwell, *Delegate:* Wolf Frees, *Female janitor:* Gwen Nelson, *Katya:* Lucy Westmore, *The train jumper:* Lili Murati, *Political officer:* Peter Madden.

FAHRENHEIT 451 (Great Britain, 1966)

Director: François Truffaut. *Producer:* Lewis M. Allen. *Associate Producer:* Michael Delamar. *Screenplay:* François Truffaut and Jean-Louis Richard. Based on the novel by Ray Bradbury. *Additional Dialogue:* David Rudkin and Helen Scott. *Photography:* Nicolas Roeg. *Editor:* Thom Noble. *Production Manager:* Ian Lewis. *Assistant Director:* Bryan Coates. *Art Director:* Syd Cain. *Special Effects:* Bowie Films, Rank Films Processing Division and Charles Staffel. *Music:* Bernard Hermann. *Design and Costume Consultant:* Tony Walton.
Production company: Anglo-Enterprise/Vineyard. *Distributed by:* Rank. *Running time:* 112 minutes. In Technicolor. Cert: A.

Montag: Oskar Werner, *Linda/Clarisse:* Julie Christie, *The Captain:* Cyril Cusack, *Fabian:* Anton Diffring, *The Man with the Apple:* Jeremy Spenser, *The Book-Woman:* Bee Duffell, *TV announcer:* Gillian Lewis, *Doris:* Ann Bell, *Helen:* Caroline Hunt, *Jackie:* Anna Palk, *The Neighbour:* Roma Milne, *The Life of Henry Brulard:* Alex Scott, *Martian Chronicles:* Dennis Gilmore, *Pride:* Fred Cox, *Prejudice:* Frank Cox, *The Pickwick Papers:* David Glover, *Machiavelli's Prince:* Michael Balfour, *Plato's Dialogues:* Judith Drynan, *The Jewish Question:* Yvonne Blake, *Weir of Hermiston:* John Rae, *Nephew of Weir of Hermiston:* Earl Younger, *1st Male Nurse:* Arthur Cox, *2nd Male Nurse:* Eric Mason, *TV announcers:* Noel Davis, Donald Pickering, *Stoneman:* Michael Mundell, *Black:* Chris Williams, *Judoka Woman:* Gillian Adam, *Judoka Man:* Edward Kaye, *1st small boy:* Mark Lester, *2nd small boy:* Kevin Elder, *Bar telephonist:* Joan Francis, *Sergeant instructor:* Tom Watson.

FAR FROM THE MADDING CROWD (Great Britain, 1967)

Director: John Schlesinger. *Producer:* Joseph Janni. *Associate Producer:* Edward Joseph. *Screenplay:* Frederic Raphael. Based on the novel by Thomas Hardy. *Photography:* Nicolas Roeg. *Editor:* Malcolm Cooke. *Production Manager:* Frank Ernst. *Assistant Director:* Kip Gowans. *Art Director:* Roy Smith. *Set Decorator:* Peter James. *Production Designer:* Richard MacDonald. *Music:* Richard Rodney Bennett, with Marcus Dods as Musical Director. *Folk Song Adviser:* Ilsa Cameron.
Production Company: Vic/Appia. *Distributed by:* Warner-Pathe. *Running time:* 168 minutes. In Technicolor Panavision 70mm. Cert: U.

Bathsheba Everdene: Julie Christie, *Sergeant Troy:* Terence Stamp, *William Boldwood:* Peter Finch, *Gabriel Oak:* Alan Bates, *Liddy:* Fiona Walker, *Fanny Robin:* Prunella Ransome, *Mrs Hurst:* Alison Leggatt, *Henery Fray:* Paul Dawkins, *Jan Coggan:* Julian Somers, *Joseph Poorgrass:* John Barrett, *Cainy Ball:* Freddie Jones, *Andrew Randle:* Andrew Robertson, *Matthew Moon:* Brian Rawlinson, *Mark Clark:* Vincent Harding, *Billy Smallbury:* Victor Stone, *Old Smallbury:* Owen Berry,

Laban Tall: Lawrence Carter, *Mrs Tall:* Pauline Melville, *Temperance:* Harriet Harper, *Soberness:* Denise Coffey, *Corporal:* Derek Ware, *Maryann Money:* Margaret Lacey, *Pennyways:* John Garrie, *Mrs Coggan:* Marie Hopps, *Labourer:* Michael Beint, *Gentleman:* Bryan Mosely, and with Walter Gale, Leslie Anderson, Keith Hooper, John Donegal, Frank Duncan and Hugh Walker.

PETULIA (Great Britain, 1968)

Director: Richard Lester. *Producer:* Raymond Wagner. *Associate Producer:* Denis O'Dell. *Executive Associate Producer:* Don Devlin. *Screenplay:* Lawrence B. Marcus. Based on the novel *Me and the Arch Kook Petulia* by John Haase. *Adaptation by:* Barbara Turner. *Photography:* Nicolas Roeg. *Editor:* Antony Gibbs. *Production Manager:* Emmett Emerson. *Assistant Director:* John Bloss. *Art Director:* Dean Tavoularis. *Production Designer:* Tony Walton. *Design Consultant:* David Hicks. *Music:* John Barry.
Production Company: Petersham Films. *Distributed by:* Warner- Pathe. *Running time:* 105 minutes. In Technicolor. Cert: X.

Petulia Danner: Julie Christie, *Archie Bollen:* George C. Scott, *David Danner:* Richard Chamberlain, *Barney:* Arthur Hill, *Polo:* Shirley Knight, *May:* Pippa Scott, *Wilma:* Kathleen Widdoes, *Warren:* Roger Bowen, *Motel receptionist:* Richard Dysart, *Nuns:* Ruth Kobart, Ellen Geer, *Mr Howard:* Lou Gilbert, *Mr Mendoza:* Nat Esformes, *Mrs Mendoza:* Maria Val, *Oliver:* Vincent Arias, *Michael:* Eric Weiss, *Stevie:* Kevin Cooper, *Mr Danner:* Joseph Cotten. *Also featured:* The Grateful Dead, Big Brother and the Holding Company, members of The Committee and members of the ATC Company.

IN SEARCH OF GREGORY (Great Britain/Italy, 1969)

Director: Peter Wood. *Producers:* Joseph Janni and Daniele Senatore. *Associate Producer:* Teddy Joseph. *Screenplay:* Tonino Guerra and Lucile Laks. *Photography:* Otto Heller and Giorgio Tonti. *Editor:* John Bloom. *Production Manager:* Carlo Lastricati. *Assistant Director:* Richard Dalton. *Art Director:* Piero Poletto. *Music:* Ron Grainer. *Songs:* 'Dreams' and 'Close' sung by Georgie Fame.
Production Company: Vic Films (London)/Vera Films (Rome). *Distributed by:* Rank. *Running time:* 90 minutes. In Technicolor. Cert: X.

Catherine Morelli: Julie Christie, *Gregory:* Michael Sarrazin, *Daniel Morelli:* John Hurt, *Max Morelli:* Adolfo Celi, *Nicole:* Paola Pitagora, *Wardle:* Roland Culver, *Taxi Driver:* Tony Selby, *Air Steward:* Jimmy Lynn, *Paquita:* Violetta Chiarini, *Encarna:* Gabriella Giorgelli, *Giselle:* Luisa de Santis, *Priest:* Ernesto Pagano, *Small boy:* Roderick Smith, *Old man:* Gordon Gostelow.

THE GO-BETWEEN (Great Britain, 1970)

Director: Joseph Losey. *Producers:* John Heyman and Norman Priggen. *Executive Producer:* Robert Velaise. *Screenplay:* Harold Pinter. Based on the novel by L.P. Hartley. *Photography:* Gerry Fisher. *Editor:* Reginald Beck. *Production Supervisor:* Denis Johnson Jr. *Assistant Director:* Richard Dalton. *Art Director:* Carmen Dillon. *Music:* Michel Legrand.
Production Company: MGM-EMI/World Film Services. *Distributed by:* MGM-EMI. *Running time:* 116 minutes. In Technicolor. Cert: AA.

Marian: Julie Christie, *Ted Burgess:* Alan Bates, *Leo Colston:* Dominic Guard, *Mrs*

Maudsley: Margaret Leighton, *Leo as an old man:* Michael Redgrave, *Mr Maudsley:* Michael Gough, *Hugh Trimingham:* Edward Fox, *Marcus:* Richard Gibson, *Denys:* Simon Hume-Kendall, *Kate:* Amaryllis Garnett, *Charles:* Roger Lloyd Pack, and with John Rees, Keith Buckley and Gordon Richardson.

McCABE AND MRS MILLER (USA, 1971)

Director: Robert Altman. *Producers:* David Foster and Mitchell Brower. *Associate Producer:* Robert Eggenweiler. *Screenplay:* Robert Altman and Brian McKay. Based on the novel *McCabe* by Edmund Naughton. *Photography:* Vilmos Zsigmond. *Editor:* Louis Lombardo. *Production Manager:* James Margellos. *2nd Unit Director:* Louis Lombardo. *Assistant Director:* Tommy Thompson. *Art Director:* Philip Thomas and Al Locatelli. *Production Designer:* Leon Ericksen. *Special Effects:* Marcel Vercoutere. *Music:* Leonard Cohen: songs sung by Leonard Cohen.
Production Company: Warner Bros. An Altman-Foster Production. *Distributed by:* Columbia-Warner. *Running time:* 121 minutes. In Technicolor Panavision. Cert: X.

John McCabe: Warren Beatty, *Constance Miller:* Julie Christie, *Sheehan:* Rene Auberjonois, *Dog Butler:* Hugh Millais, *Ida Coyle:* Shelley Duvall, *Sears:* Michael Murphy, *Smalley:* John Schuck, *Mr Elliott:* Corey Fischer, *The lawyer:* William Devane, *Bart Coyle:* Bert Remsen, *Cowboy:* Keith Carradine, *Bread:* Jace Vander Veen, *Kid:* Manfred Schulz, *Lily:* Jackie Crossland, *Kate:* Elizabeth Murphy, *Blanche:* Linda Sorenson, *Birdie:* Elizabeth Knight, *Maisie:* Maysie Hoy, *Ruth:* Linda Kupecek, *Eunice:* Janet Wright, *Alma:* Carey Lee McKenzie, *Hollander:* Anthony Holland, *Archer:* Tom Hill, *Jeremy:* Berg J. Newson, *Bartenders:* Wayne Robson, Wayne Grace, *Riley Quinn:* Jack Riley, *Town drunk:* Robert Fortier, *Shorty Dunn:* Wesley Taylor, *Mrs Dunn:* Anne Cameron, *Bill Cubbs:* Graeme Campbell, *J.J.:* J.S. Johnson, *Joe Sortreed:* Joe Clarke, *Andy Anderson:* Harry Frazier, *Gilchrist:* Edwin Collier, *Quigley:* Terence Kelly, *Fiddler:* Brantley F. Kearns, *Buffalo:* Don Francks, *Sumner Washington:* Rodney Gage, *Mrs Washington:* Lili Francks, and with Joan McGuire, Harvey Lowe, Eric Scheider, Milos Zatovic, Claudine Melgrave, Derek Deurvorst, Alexander Diakun and Gordon Robertson as the townspeople.

DON'T LOOK NOW (Great Britain/Italy, 1973)

Director: Nicolas Roeg. *Producer:* Peter Katz. *Executive Producer:* Anthony B. Unger. *Associate Producer:* Federico Mueller. *Screenplay:* Allan Scott and Chris Bryant. Based on the short story by Daphne du Maurier. *Photography:* Anthony Richmond. *Editor:* Graeme Clifford. *Production Manager:* Franco Coduti. *Assistant Director:* Francesco Cinieri. *Art Director:* Giovanni Soccol. *Music:* Pino D'Onnagio, with Giampiero Boneschi as Musical Director.
Production Company: Casey Productions (London)/Eldorado Films (Rome). *Distributed by:* British Lion. *Running time:* 110 minutes. In Technicolor. Cert: X.

Laura Baxter: Julie Christie, *John Baxter:* Donald Sutherland, *Heather:* Hilary Mason, *Wendy:* Clelia Matania, *Bishop Barbarrigo:* Massimo Serato, *Inspector Longhi:* Renato Scarpa, *Workman:* Giorgio Trestini, *Hotel manager:* Leopoldo Trieste, *Anthony Babbage:* David Tree, *Mandy Babbage:* Ann Rye, *Johnny Baxter:* Nicholas Salter, *Christine Baxter:* Sharon Williams, *Detective Sabbione:* Bruno Cattaneo, *Dwarf:* Adelina Poerio.

SHAMPOO (USA, 1975)

Director: Hal Ashby. *Producer:* Warren Beatty. *Associate Producer and Production Manager:* Charles H. Maguire. *Screenplay:* Robert Towne and Warren Beatty.

Photography: Laszlo Kovacs. *Editor:* Robert Jones. *Assistant Directors:* Art Levinson and Ron Wright. *Production Designer:* Richard Sylbert. *Art Director:* Stu Campbell. *Set Designers:* Robert Resh and Charles Zacha. *Music:* Paul Simon, with orchestration by Pat Williams.
Production Company: Persky-Bright/Vista. A Rubeeker Production. *Distributed by:* Columbia-Warner. *Running time:* 110 minutes. In Technicolor. Cert: X.

George: Warren Beatty, *Jackie Shawn:* Julie Christie, *Jill Haynes:* Goldie Hawn, *Felicia Karpf:* Lee Grant, *Lester Karpf:* Jack Warden, *Johnny Pope:* Tony Bill, *Lorna:* Carrie Fisher, *Norman:* Jay Robinson, *Mr Pettis:* George Furth, *Tina:* Jaye P. Morgan, *Mary:* Ann Weldon, *Dennis:* Randy Scheer, *Gloria:* Susanna Moore, *Ricci:* Mike Olton, *Devra:* Luana Anders, *Senator East:* Brad Dexter, *Sid Roth:* William Castle, *Izzy:* Jack Bernardi, *Rosalind:* Doris Packer, *Kenneth:* Hal Buckley, *Red Dog:* Howard Hesseman, *Girl on Sunset Strip:* Michelle Phillips, *Girl in car:* Cheri Latimer, *Girl on street:* Susan Blakely.

DEMON SEED (USA, 1977)

Director: Donald Cammell. *Producer:* Herb Jaffe. *Associate Producer:* Steven C. Jaffe. *Screenplay:* Robert Jaffe and Roger O. Hirson. Based on the novel by Dean R. Koontz. *Photography:* Bill Butler. *Editor:* Frank Mazzola. *Production Manager:* Michael Rachmil. *Assistant Directors:* Edward Teets and Alan Brimfield. *Production Designer:* Edward Carfagno. *Set Decorator:* Barbara Krieger. *Special Effects:* Tom Fisher. *Mechanical Special Effects:* Glen Robinson. *Video Coordinator:* Dixie J. Capp. *Synthavision Animation:* Bo Gehring. *Tetralinks:* Level-Seven. *Delta Wing Computer Animation:* Computer Science Department, University of Utah. *Electronic Visuals:* Ron Hays. *Electronic Animation:* Richard L. Froman. *Genigraphics Animation:* Grant Bassett. *Aerial Photography:* MacGillivray- Freeman. *Special Proteus monitor footage:* Jordan Belson. *Music:* Jerry Fielding. *Costumes:* Sandy Cole.
Production Company: MGM. *Distributed by:* CIC. *Running time:* 95 minutes. In Metrocolor Panavision. Cert: AA.

Dr Susan Harris: Julie Christie, *Dr Alex Harris:* Fritz Weaver, *Walter Gabler:* Gerrit Graham, *Petrosian:* Berry Kroeger, *Dr Soon Yen:* Lisa Lu, *Cameron:* Larry J. Blake, *Royce:* John O'Leary, *Mokri:* Alfred Dennis, *Warner:* David Roberts, *Mrs Talbert:* Patricia Wilson, *Night operator:* E. Hampton Beagle, *Technicians:* Michael Glass, Barbara O. Jones, *Amy:* Dana Laurita, *Joan Kemp:* Monica MacLean, *Scientist:* Harold Oblong, *Maria, the housekeeper:* Georgie Paul, *Marlene:* Michelle Stacy, *Babies:* Tiffany Potter, Felix Silla.

HEAVEN CAN WAIT (USA, 1978)

Directors: Warren Beatty and Buck Henry. *Producer:* Warren Beatty. *Executive Producers:* Howard W. Koch Jr., and Charles H. Maguire. *Screenplay:* Elaine May and Warren Beatty. Based on the play by Harry Segall. *Photography:* William A. Fraker. *Editors:* Robert C. Jones and Don Zimmerman. *Production Manager:* Charles H. Maguire. *Assistant Directors:* Howard W. Koch Jr., and Craig Huston. *Production Designer:* Paul Sylbert. *Art Director:* Edwin O'Donovan. *Special effects:* Robert MacDonald. *Music:* Dave Grusin. *Songs:* 'Sonata No. 3' by G.F. Handel, performed by Paul Brodie and Antonin Kubalek; 'The Rams Marching Song' by John T. Boudreau; 'Entry of the Gladiators' by Julius Fucik; 'Happy Birthday to You' by Mildren J. Hill and Patty S. Hill; 'Ciribiribin' by Albert Pestalozza. *Costumes:* Richard Bruno. *Technical Consultants:* Les Josephson and Frank O'Neill.
Production Company: Shelburne Associates for Paramount. *Distributed by:* CIC.

Running time: 101 minutes. Movielab colour. Cert: A.

Joe Pendleton: Warren Beatty, *Betty Logan:* Julie Christie, *Mr Jordan:* James Mason, *Max Corkle:* Jack Warden, *Tony Abbott:* Charles Grodin, *Julia Farnsworth:* Dyan Cannon, *The Escort:* Buck Henry, *Krim:* Vincent Gardenia, *Sisk:* Joseph Maher, *Bentley:* Hamilton Camp, *Lavinia:* Jeannie Linero, *Everett:* Arthur Malet, *Corinne:* Stephanie Faracy, *Gardener:* Harry D.K. Wong, *Security Guard:* George J. Manos, *Peters:* Larry Block, *Conway:* Frank Campanella, *Tomarken:* Bill Sorrells, *TV interviewer:* Dick Enberg, *Head coach:* Dolph Sweet, *General manager:* R.G. Armstrong, *Trainer:* Ed V. Peck, *Former owner:* John Randolph, *Adviser to former owner:* Richard O'Brien, *Haitian ambassador:* Joseph F. Makel, *Team doctor:* Will Hare, *Way Station attendant:* Lee Weaver, *Newspaperman:* Roger Bowen, *Oppenheim:* Keene Curtis, *Renfield:* William Larsen, *Middleton:* Morgan Farley, *Lawson:* William Bogert, *Board members:* Robert E. Leonard, Joel Marston, Earl Montgomery, Robert C. Stevens, *Coliseum security guard:* Bernie Massa, *Reporter:* Peter Tomarken, *Nuclear reporter:* William Sylvester, *Woman reporter:* Lisa Blake Richards, *Highwire performer:* Charlie Charles, *Chauffeur:* Nick Outin, *Hodges:* Jerry Scanlan, *Kowalsky:* Jim Boeke, *Gudnitz:* Marvin Fleming, *Gorman:* Deacon Jones, *Owens:* Les Josephson, *Cassidy:* Jack T. Snow, *TV commentator:* Curt Gowdy, *TV colour analyst:* Al DeRogatis.

SOPHIE AND THE CAPTAIN (France, 1978)

Director: Liliane De Kermadec. *Executive Producer:* Irene Silberman.
Film starring Julie Christie cancelled after two weeks shooting.

MEMOIRS OF A SURVIVOR (Great Britain, 1981)

Director: David Gladwell. *Producers:* Michael Medwin and Penny Clark. *Associate Producer:* Michael Guest. *Screenplay:* Kerry Crabbe and David Gladwell. Based on the novel *The Memoirs of a Survivor* by Doris Lessing. *Photography:* Walter Lassally. *Editor:* William Shapter. *Location Supervisor:* Robin Douet. *2nd Unit Photography:* Roger Deakins. *Assistant Directors:* Peter Price, Peter Cotton and Tim Reed. *Production Designer:* Keith Wilson. *Art Director Asst:* Denis Bosher. *Set Dresser:* Simon Wakefield. *Special Effects:* Effects Associates. *Music:* Mike Thorn. *Costumes:* Based on an idea by Helen Turner. *Wardrobe Supervisor:* Richard Pointing.
Production Company: Memorial Films. In association with the National Film Finance Corporation, EMI Films. *Distributed by:* Columbia-EMI-Warner. *Running time:* 115 minutes. In Technicolor. Cert: X.

"D": Julie Christie, *Gerald:* Christopher Guard, *Emily Mary Cartwright:* Leonie Mellinger, *June:* Debbie Hutchings, *Victorian Father:* Nigel Hawthorne, *Victorian Mother:* Pat Keen, *Victorian Emily:* Georgina Griffiths, *Victorian Son:* Christopher Tsangarides, *Newsvendor/gardener:* Mark Dignam, *Janet White:* Alison Dowling, *Professor White:* John Franklyn-Robbins, *Mrs White:* Rowena Cooper, *Woman on waste ground:* Barbara Hicks, *Man delivering Emily:* John Cromer, *Maureen:* Adrienne Byrne, *Sandra:* Marion Owen Smith, *Jill:* Tara MacGowran, *Neighbours:* Jeanne Watts, Pamela Cundell, Bryan Matheson, *Victorian nurse:* Ann Tirard, *Woman at news stand:* Jeillo Edwards, *Men at news stand:* Arthur Lovegrove, John Ruthland, and with children from Anna Scher Theatre Management as Orphan and Underground children.

LES QUARANTIEMES RUGISSANTS (France/West Germany/Sierra Leone, 1982)

Director: Christian de Chalonge. *Producer:* Perrine Pavie. *Executive Producer:* Christian Ferry. *Screenplay:* Andre G. Brunelin. From a story idea by Brunelin,

Perrin and de Chalonge, based on *The Last Strange Voyage of Donald Crowhurst* by Ron Hall and Nicolas Tomalin. *Photography:* Luciano Tovoli. *Editor:* Henri Lanoe. *Nautical Advisers:* Eric Tabarly and Bernard Deguy. *French Navy Adviser:* Pierre Dubrulle. *Production Manager:* Gerard Crosnier. *2nd Unit Director:* Bernard Bolzinger. *2nd Unit Photography:* Patrick Blossier. *Sierra Leone camera sequences:* Jean Penzer. *Music:* Henri Lanoe.
Production Company: TF 1 Films Production/Gaumont coproduction in association with Tele-Munchen (Munich) and Sierra Leone Television. *Distributed by:* Gaumont. *Running time:* 132 minutes. In colour.

Julien Dantec: Jacques Perrin, *Catherine Dantec:* Julie Christie, *Barral:* Michel Serrault.

THE RETURN OF THE SOLDIER (Great Britain, 1982)

Director: Alan Bridges. *Producers:* Ann Skinner and Simon Relph. *Executive Producers:* Edward Simons, Barry R. Cooper, John Quested and J. Gordon Arnold. *Screenplay:* Hugh Whitemore. Based on the novel by Rebecca West. *Photography:* Stephen Goldblatt. *Editor:* Laurence Mery Clark. *Production Manager:* Redmond Morris. *Location Manager:* Guy Travers. *Assistant Director:* Allan James, with Peter Waller and Michael Zimbrich. *Production Designer:* Luciana Arrighi. *Art Director:* Ian Whittaker. *Special Effects:* Nick Allder. *Music:* Richard Rodney Bennett, with Marcus Dods as Musical Director. *Costumes:* Shirley Russell.
Production Company: Brent Walker Pictures/Barry R. Cooper Productions. In association with Skreba Films. *Distributed by:* 20th Century-Fox. *Running time:* 102 minutes. In Technicolor. Cert: PG (A).

Captain Chris Baldry: Alan Bates, *Jenny:* Ann-Margaret, *Margaret Grey:* Glenda Jackson, *Kitty Baldry:* Julie Christie, *Frank:* Jeremy Kemp, *Edward:* Edward De Souza, *William Grey:* Frank Finlay, *Brigadier:* Jack May, *Dr Gilbert Anderson:* Ian Holm, *Young Jenny:* Emily Irvin, *Young Chris:* William Booker, *Emery:* Elizabeth Edmonds, *Ward:* Hilary Mason, *Pearson:* John Sharp, *Ballerina:* Valerie Aitken, *Alexandra:* Amanda Grinling, *Young Civilian Gentleman:* Nicholas Frankau, *1st Young Officer:* Robin Langford, *2nd Young Officer:* Stephen Finlay, *Lord Lieutenant:* Llewellyn Rees, *Ballerina's boyfriend:* Jeremy Arnold, *Pianist at Party:* Alan Corduner, *Groom:* John Lonsdale, *Chauffeur:* Robert Keegan, *Girl searching in hospital:* Pauline Quirke, *Sister:* Sheila Keith, *Downstairs nurse:* Cathy Finlay, *Weeping man:* Charles Morgan, *Ward sister:* Shirley Caine, *Ward nurse:* Gerry Cowper, *Wounded officer:* Patrick Gordon, *Delivery man:* Larry Noble, *Beatrice:* Valerie Whittington, and with Stephen Whittaker, Kevin Whately, Patsy Byrne, Michael Cochrane, Vickery Turner, Dorothy Alison, Norman Mitchell, Martin Ransley and Jane Laurie.

HEAT AND DUST (Great Britain, 1982)

Director: James Ivory. *Producer:* Ismail Merchant. *Associate Producers:* Rita Mangat and Connie Kaiserman. *Screenplay:* Ruth Prawer Jhabvala. Based on her own novel. *Urdu Dialogue:* Saeed Jaffrey. *Hindi Dialogue:* Harish Khare. *Photography:* Walter Lassally. *Assistant Photography:* Tony Garrett, Rajesh Joshi. *Editor:* Humphrey Dixon, assisted by Mark Potter Jnr. *Production Coordinator:* Shama Habibullah. *Production Manager:* Peter Manley. *Location Manager:* Deepak Nayar. *Assistant Director:* Kevan Baker, with David Nichols and Gopal Ram. *Production Designer:* Wilfred Shingleton. *Art Directors:* Maurice Fowler and Ram Yadekar. *Set Dresser:*

Agnes Fernandes. *Music:* Richard Robbins, with Zakir Hussain as associate. *Singer:* Ameer Mohammed Khan. *Costumes:* Barbara Lane.
Production Company: Merchant Ivory Productions. *Distributed by:* Enterprise. *Running time:* 130 minutes. In colour. Cert: 15 (AA)

(In the 1920s: the Civil Lines at Satipur) Douglas Rivers: Christopher Cazenove, *Olivia Rivers:* Greta Scacchi, *Mr Crawford:* Julian Glover, *Mrs Crawford:* Susan Fleetwood, *Dr Saunders:* Patrick Godfrey, *Mrs Saunders:* Jennifer Kendal.
(The Palace in Khatm) The Nawab: Shashi Kapoor, *The Begum:* Madhur Jaffrey, *Harry:* Nickolas Grace, *Major Minnies:* Barry Foster, *Lady Mackleworth:* Amanda Walker, *Chief Princess:* Sudha Chopra, *Dacoit Chief:* Sajid Khan, *Guy:* Daniel Chatto.
(The 1980s: in Satipur Town) Anne: Julie Christie, *Inder Lal:* Zakir Hussain, *Rita, Inder Lal's wife:* Ratna Pathak, *Inder Lal's mother:* Tarla Mehta, *Chidananda, 'Chid':* Charles McCaughan, *Maji:* Parveen Paul, *Dr Gopal:* Jayant Kripilani, *Leelavati:* Leelabhai.

SEPARATE TABLES (Great Britain, 1983)

Director: John Schlesinger. *Producers:* Patrick Dromgoole and Mort Abrahams. *Associate Producer:* Danny Steinmann. *HTV Studio Director:* Ken Price. *Written by:* Terence Rattigan. *Production Design:* Julia Trevelyan Oman. *Staging by:* Cyril Bennett. *Cameras:* Gary Penny. *Lighting Director:* John Burgess. *Vision Controllers:* Peter Wherlock and Tony Poole. *Vision Mixer:* John Bourne. *Stage Manager:* Christopher Lloyd Pack. *Art Designer:* Chris Cook. *Production Controller:* Dave Bartle. *Floor Manager:* Tony Annis. *Videotape Editor:* Peter Buchanan. *Casting:* Noel Davis. *Music:* Schubert Impromptu Opus 90 No 3 in G; performed by Philip Smith. *Costumes:* Jane Robinson.
Production Company: An HTV Production in association with Edie & Ely, London and Primetime Television. Colour. Television distribution.

Mrs Anne Shankland, Miss Sybil Railton-Bell: Julie Christie, *Mr Malcolm, Major Pollock:* Alan Bates, *Miss Cooper:* Claire Bloom, *Mrs Railton-Bell:* Irene Worth, *Lady Matheson:* Sylvia Barter, *Mr Fowler:* Bernard Archard, *Miss Meacham:* Liz Smith, *Mabel:* Kathy Staff, *Charles Stratton:* Brian Deacon, *Miss Jean Tanner:* Susannah Fellows, *Doreen:* Chrissie Cotterill.

THE GOLD DIGGERS (Great Britain, 1984)

Director: Sally Potter. *Screenplay:* Sally Potter, Rose English and Lindsay Cooper. *Photography:* Babette Mangolte. *Editor:* Sally Potter. *Art Director:* Rose English. *Sound:* Diana Rushton. *Music:* Lindsay Cooper.
Production Company: British Film Institute. *Running time:* 87 minutes. In black & white (35mm).

With Julie Christie, Colette Laffont, Jacky Lansley, Hilary Westlake and David Gale.

Julie Christie briefly participated in two additional film productions: *Tonite Let's All Make Love in London,* a swingin' 1967 documentary, and Robert Altman's major feature *Nashville* (1975) in which she guested, as herself, along with Elliott Gould.

INDEX